Deep Church Rising

Recovering the Roots of
Christian Orthodoxy

ANDREW G. WALKER
and
ROBIN A. PARRY

Published in the United States of America in 2014
as *Deep Church Rising: The Third Schism and the Recovery of Christian Orthodoxy*
by Cascade Books, an imprint of Wipf and Stock Publishers, Eugene, Oregon

First published in Great Britain in 2014

Society for Promoting Christian Knowledge
36 Causton Street
London SW1P 4ST
www.spckpublishing.co.uk

British Library Cataloguing-in-Publication Data
A catalogue record for this book is available from the British Library

ISBN 978–0–281–07272–9
eBook ISBN 978–0–281–07273–6

First printed in Great Britain by Ashford Colour Press
Subsequently digitally printed in Great Britain

Produced on paper from sustainable forests

Andrew would like to dedicate this book to
Richard Chartres, Bishop of London

Robin would like to dedicate this book to
John Inge, Bishop of Worcester
and
Denise Inge (1963–2014),
an inspirational and extraordinary Christian woman

"May the good teaching of our fathers who met at Nicea shine forth again, so that doxology which is in harmony with saving baptism [i.e., with Matt 28:19] may be duly offered to the Blessed Trinity."

—BASIL OF CAESAREA (*EP.* 91, WRITTEN IN 372 AD)

Contents

"It is only when we know something of our roots that we are able to move and explore without the feverish longing to be stimulated – or the anxious fear that we are betraying something, though we don't actually know what. We don't become either human or holy without the nurture and wisdom of others; this book helps us to make contact with those others so that we can indeed grow in humanity, sanctity, and discernment as we need to."

—ROWAN WILLIAMS
MASTER OF MAGDELENE COLLEGE, CAMBRIDGE
AND AUTHOR OF *BEING CHRISTIAN* AND OTHER BOOKS

"*Deep Church Rising* is a deep book, intrepidly and winsomely demonstrating the ongoing viability of orthodoxy."

—RODNEY CLAPP, AUTHOR OF
*TORTURED WONDERS: CHRISTIAN SPIRITUALITY
FOR PEOPLE, NOT ANGELS* AND OTHER BOOKS

"This book, written with punctilious scholarship, vast scope, fidelity to history, and, perhaps above all, with great gracefulness, calls the churches to a sober scrutiny of themselves, and, perhaps thence, to fundamental reflection on what the church is. I am immensely taken with this book."

—THOMAS HOWARD, AUTHOR OF
ON BEING CATHOLIC AND OTHER BOOKS

Preface

Andrew

This book is a reflection of the debates of an informal network of Christians in Greater London that regularly met in St Paul's Church, Hammersmith, and King's College, London, from 2006 to 2008. Four people were responsible for setting up this group: Simon Downham, who generously offered us hospitality at St Paul's, where he was the incumbent vicar; Ian Stackhouse, former leader in the "new church" sector and now pastor of Millmead Baptist Church in Guildford; my former colleague at King's College, Luke Bretherton, who is now Professor of Christian Ethics at Duke University; and myself, now Emeritus Professor of Theology, Culture, and Education at King's College London. Participants were mainly evangelicals who had some involvement in the Charismatic Movement (although we did have church leaders from other constituencies who came from time to time). Luke Bretherton suggested we should refer to the seminars as a "conversation" and after some six months of discussion I raised the issue that the "conversation" was about method but we needed to define the *content*. And so I suggested C. S. Lewis's alternative phrase for "mere Christianity," "deep church."

In 1985, after the publication of the first edition of my sociological study on what were then called house churches, I decided that all my future publications, academic and popular, would reflect my Christian commitments and concerns. So in a sense I turned from poacher (sociologist of religion) to gamekeeper (applied theologian). I did this because I was troubled—and remain so—at the lack of knowledge and confidence that Western Christians have in the Christian tradition. With the backing of my bishop, Metropolitan Anthony, and under the patronage of the then Archbishop of Canterbury (now Lord Carey), I founded and directed The C. S. Lewis Centre for the study of religion and modernity from 1987 to 1995. We were not a Lewis fan club but an international research organization dedicated to "mere Christianity," which we understood to be a defense of historical and Trinitarian orthodoxy. This defense reflected a wide spectrum of churchmanship and scholarship. For example, in an early collection of original articles we had a letter of support from the Vatican, a foreword by Dr. Billy Graham (Baptist), and contributors included Professor Colin Gunton (United Reformed Church), Professor Gavin D'Costa (Roman Catholic), Professor Keith Ward (Anglican), Professor Thomas F. Torrance (Presbyterian), Cardinal Suenens (Roman Catholic), and Metropolitan Anthony (Orthodox)

In the early 1990s, after a direct approach from Bishop Lesslie Newbigin, I threw in my lot with the Gospel and Culture movement and our two organizations formally merged for the period between 1995 and 1997. Like myself Lesslie was dismayed at the way in which so many churches had thrown in the towel to modernity, which had thrown down the gauntlet to religious faith (the challenge was an amalgam of secularist ideologies and what sociologists have called secularization—a process of disenchantment with religious faith). Churches were increasingly removed from the "public square" and shunted into a world of leisure and voluntary association where truth was downgraded to private beliefs or mere opinion. Lesslie was particularly attached to the idea that the gospel was public truth and never did accept the separation of fact from value, which has been such a feature of the modern world.

Both Lesslie and I were convinced ecumenists but traditional in our beliefs. Lesslie used to say we should start at the center of Christian faith— that Jesus is Lord—and stick to the central tenants of the gospel to find true unity. My conviction is that we have fallen foul of false divisions in the churches and have separated or broken things that should stay together. This is not to deny the very real divisions that have occurred among Christians but it is a stance that refuses to opt for a faith that pits Bible against tradition, enthusiasm against contemplation, catholicity against gathered remnants, individual believer against church. In Part One of this book we have not shied away from the great schisms of Christendom but we do insist that they are somewhat relativized by what we call the third schism. The third schism—unlike the split between the Orthodox East and the Catholic West and between Protestants and Catholics in the Reformation in the West—undermines the very basis of Christian faith in its denial of the Trinity, incarnation, and the resurrection, and in its treating Scripture as an object of scientific inquiry rather than as a sacred text.

Above all this is a book about recovering the gospel. This recovery is essential for the future of the church and the world: we are not going to be saved by a purpose-driven church or any gnostic substitute—the power of positive thinking *a la* Norman Vincent Peale looms ever larger in our consumer-driven society. In order to recover the gospel we have to find the church. Ecclesiology is the Achilles heel of Evangelicalism. When we have put missiology back where it belongs—in the church—we will discover the true source of mission and truth. But our confidence in the gospel as the foundation of faith and the source of conversion is not a model of success. We are the bearers and keepers of the flame: in short we are called to be faithful disciples, not conquerors.

Robin

I, along with many others, was introduced to the notion of "deep church" through Andrew Walker. Andrew is one of the Orthodox thinkers that evangelicals, especially in the UK, gravitate toward. Indeed, for many years he has made it something of his mission to help evangelicals to draw deeply from the Great Tradition while remaining true to their evangelical and charismatic instincts. As a charismatic evangelical I was already well aware that we should not set the Word against the Spirit, the evangelical against the charismatic. What Andrew taught me was that the big mistake of many evangelicals is to set *tradition* up in conflict with the Word or with the Spirit. Tradition is too often seen by evangelicals as "the dead words of men" to be opposed in the name of the inspired words of Scripture and the living activity of the Spirit. "Tradition kills," we say, "but the Word and the Spirit bring life." This conflict approach is a very unhelpful way to think about the relationship between the Spirit, tradition, and Scripture. For Andrew—who is committed to the authority of the Bible and still testifies unflinchingly to his own powerful charismatic encounter—tradition, Scripture, and the Spirit form a threefold cord that should not be untwisted. That insight has been transformative for me and for many other British evangelicals I know. It also underlies the approach of this book.

Over the years Andrew has published various articles and books that have circled around the challenges posed by modernity and postmodernity for the church and its mission. Increasingly he has been emphasizing the central role of recovering deep church. For about ten years I have been encouraging Andrew to offer a more sustained exploration of deep church, beginning with the notion of the third schism and moving on to explore deep church as the authentic Christian mode of response to it. Andrew, however, has been suffering for the past few years with Parkinson's disease and it has become increasingly clear that such a project was simply not realistic. Yet my belief in a deep church vision and my gut instinct that such a book ought to be out there did not wane. Thus it was that Andrew and I decided to write the book together.

What we offer here are a set of reflections that represent a deep church approach to contemporary Christian belief, worship, and living. But notice that I say "*a* deep church approach," not *the* deep church approach. We speak on our own behalf and not on behalf of others committed to ancient-future faith (whether they be individuals or denominations). We do not even speak on behalf of the Deep Church network that existed in London. Those who share with us the basic commitment to the importance of holding fast to classical orthodoxy may well disagree with us on some issues. That's fair enough. We offer these thoughts for consideration and discussion and not as a final word. Nevertheless, what you find here is the most thorough and sustained attempt made so far by Andrew or myself to spell out what we mean by "a deep church vision." We offer it to the church as it struggles to navigate that fine and difficult route between the Scylla of cultural irrelevance and the Charybdis of compromising the "faith once for all delivered to the saints." To chart that perilous course we need Spirit, Scripture, and tradition, as well as great discernment in understanding the cultural contexts in which we find ourselves. This is a task that needs all the diverse skills of the crew and all hands on deck. Our book does not map the path but rather gestures, perhaps a little wildly at times, in the general direction of travel. It also points out a few whirlpools, hidden rocks, and sea monsters on the way. Our prayer is that we may inspire some of our readers, and others through them, to sail with wisdom, courage, and eyes fixed on the horizon, on the author and perfecter of our faith, Christ Jesus.

Acknowledgments

Chapter 1 contains modified versions of long extracts from:

Andrew G. Walker, "The Third Schism: The Great Divide in Christianity Today." In *In Search of Christianity*, edited by Tony Moss, 202–17. London: Firethorn, 1986.

Andrew G. Walker, "Recovering Deep Church: Theological and Spiritual Renewal." In *Remembering Our Future: Explorations in Deep Church*, edited by Andrew G. Walker and Luke Bretherton, 1–29. Milton Keynes, UK: Paternoster, 2007.

Chapter 3 is a modified version of:

Andrew G. Walker, "Deep Church as *Paradosis:* On Relating Scripture and Tradition." In *Remembering Our Future: Explorations in Deep Church*, edited by Andrew G. Walker and Luke Bretherton, 59–80. Milton Keynes, UK: Paternoster, 2007.

Abbreviations

1 *Apol.*	Justin Martyr, *Apologia 1* (*First Apology*)
Bap.	Theodore of Mopsuestia, *Liber ad Baptizandos* (*Baptismal Homilies*)
Cat.	Cyril of Jerusalem, *Catechetical Lectures*
Comm.	Vincent of Lérins, *Commonitorium* (*Commonitory*)
Conf.	Augustine, *Confessionum libri XIII* (*Confessions*)
Dem.	Irenaeus, *Adversus hearesus* (*Against Heresies*)
de Sp. sanct.	Basil, *Liber de Spiritu sancto* (*On the Holy Spirit*)
Did.	*Didache*
Diogn.	*Epistle to Diognetus*
ep.	*Epistulae* (*Letters*)
Fund.	Augustine, *Contra epistulam Manichaei quam vocant Fumdamenti* (*Against the Letter of the Manichaeans That They Call the "Basics"*)
Haer.	Irenaeus, *Adversus haeresus* (*Against Heresies*)
Hom. in Heb.	John Chrysostom, *Homiliae in epistulam ad Hebraeos* (*Homily on the Epistle to the Hebrews*)
Hom. Jo.	John Chrysostom, *Homiliae in Joannem* (*Homily on John*)
Ign. *Eph.*	Ignatius, *To the Ephesians*
Ign. *Smyrn.*	Ignatius, *To the Smyrnaeans*
Ign. *Trall.*	Ignatius, *To the Trallians*
Myst.	Cyril of Jerusalem, *Mystagōgikai* (*Mystagogic Catecheses*)
Pan.	Epiphanius, *Panarion* (*Adversus hearesus*) (*Refutation of All Heresies*)
m. Pesaḥ	*Pesaḥim* (in the Mishnah)
Praescr.	Tertullian, *De praescriptione haereticorum* (*Prescription against Heretics*)
Princ.	Origen, *De principiis* (*Peri archōn*) (*First Principles*)
Ortho.	John of Damascus, *Ekdosis akribes tēs Orthodoxou Pisteos* (*An Exact Exposition of the Orthodox Faith*)
Vit. Ant.	Athanasius, *Vita Antonii* (*Life of Anthony*)

PART ONE

The Third Schism:
On Losing the Gospel

INTRODUCTION

The Third Schism and Deep Church

CHRISTIANITY IS NOW ON sale in multiform shapes and sizes. Competing in the open market with other religions, there is a bewildering yet broad choice of "real" and "best" Christianities for anyone who wants to buy. No doubt someone will soon publish *The Consumer Guide to God* so that people can pop in and out of churches with the same ease and comfort as they visit their favorite restaurants.

"You pays your money and takes your choice" surely exemplifies the "spirit of the age"; for in our culture religion is not seen as the *raison d'être* of our society and life: it is a series of options that we choose—or goods that we buy—if we feel so inclined. This plurality of religious belief and practice is often applauded as evidence of cultural maturity and tolerance. Nobody forces a version on us any more. There are many varieties on sale vying for our attention, but we, the consumers, have the absolute power of either buying one version in preference to another or withholding payment altogether.

In this sense, of course, we have to admit to being just part of the crowd like everybody else. While we accept the inevitability of this, and while we run the logical risk of being hoist by our own petard, we want to assert in this introduction that the Christian gospel has a central core of truth that has an objective character about it. Christian faith is not like a lump of clay that we can reshape however we see fit. While it comes in many shapes and sizes they represent variations on a theme, sharing a common root in the apostolic witness to Jesus maintained by the community of the church. It is, in other words, not infinitely malleable but has a "this and not that" character.

The purpose of this assertion, however, is not so that we can demonstrate this objectivity in a logical way, but in order that we can make out a plausible case that the Christianity of the historic church, of the ancient creeds, and sacred scriptural canons needs to be on guard against being swallowed by something else in the name of religious progress; of capitulating to a different gospel.

To say this is to come clean and admit two things. First, that we are traditionalists or primitivists of sorts, and believe that the Christian faith is founded on biblical revelations concerning a loving God and his incarnation in the world through the historical person of Jesus Christ. Such a belief takes some swallowing today, or in any age, and cannot be demonstrated as factual in a scientific or empirical way. After all, God as traditionally conceived by Christians is not simply a being, not even the *Supreme* Being, alongside or on the same plane as other beings. The church has usually sought to maintain that God's reality is of a *fundamentally different order* from anything in creation. God dwells "in light inaccessible, hid from our eyes," and simply *cannot* be studied by scientific or other empirical methods. So, for instance, while historians may indeed be able to offer insights on the historical Jesus they will simply be unable to declare *in their capacity as historians* whether Jesus really was God incarnate. How could one empirically assess *that*? This is not to say, however, that such a belief is false, and certainly it is not to say that it is irrational. It is simply to say that there are some aspects of reality that are beyond the limits of scientific rationality and method. (It should go without saying that this is no threat to science, only to scient*ism*, the ideology that all truth claims about the world can be assessed by the sciences.)

The second thing to admit is that we are not approaching this introduction from an Empyrean vantage point nor with the logical disinterest of a mathematical calculator. Christianity, the religion of the apostles, tattered and divided as it is by schism and heresy—but still bearing the marks of God's grace—has very gradually over the past four hundred years entered what is one of the most serious tests of its two-thousand-year history. We passionately want to see that faith both survive and strengthen in the face of modern Christian alternatives.

We have chosen, therefore, polemic rather than a careful historical analysis as the medium to express both passion and conviction. The polemic—that Christendom has entered its third and most serious schism—is, we believe, true, and is based on historical argument that is rational and open to refutation. As to whether the schism is a good or a bad thing, that depends on which side of the present divide you stand.

To say that we are dealing with a protracted crisis in Christendom, which can be characterized as a third schism, necessitates a brief mention of the first two divides, and something about the meaning of schism. "Schism" is a word that we usually associate with a breach in the unity of the visible church. The so-called Great Western Schism of 1378–1417, for example, was a break in the unity of the (Western) Catholic Church due to disputed elections to the papacy in which, until the schism was healed, there were competing popes.

As serious a schism as this was, however, it was not of the magnitude of the really great divides of Christendom. Furthermore, the word "schism" means to divide, cleave, or rend. It is *this* more general sense of major division with which we are concerned rather than the idea of a *visible* split. The first two great schisms of Christianity, between the Eastern and Western churches, and the Western Reformation, were indeed visible divides. The third schism, because it cuts across denominations rather than between them, is not invisible (we can see it happening), but it is not yet denomination against denomination creating visible and separate camps within Christendom. In that sense it differs from the other schisms.

The First Schism: The Divide between the Western and Eastern Churches

It says a great deal for our parochial worldview that Christianity is seen as a Western religion. Western students of theology take some time to adjust to the fact that the Western Reformation is only part of a far more fundamental divide of the Christian church. This division has its origins in the inability of the Greek East and Latin West to cohere.

Although the official date of the Great Schism is 1054, this is too simplistic. In reality the two halves of Christendom had been pulling apart for centuries. The unilateral addition by the Latin West of the word *filioque* ("and the Son") to the Nicene creed (which now said of the Holy Spirit, "who proceeds from the Father *and the Son*") and the decision by the Roman See that the Bishop there was to be seen no longer as *Primus inter pares* (the first among equals) but as possessing superior and unique authority in the Christian church, are the main reasons cited by Eastern Catholics (the Orthodox) for the Great Schism (see Appendix 1).

This is not untrue, but it is also the case that the nature of spirituality, liturgy, and theology increasingly developed along separate lines as Eastern and Western cultures evolved and diverged.

Henceforth the Orthodox continued without Pope and without reformation (to this day), and the Catholic Church—cut off from the collegiality of the Eastern sister churches—went it alone in an increasingly centralized and Westernized way. The essential tragedy of the schism was that the universal catholicity of the "one undivided church" was broken.

The council of Florence in 1438–39 looked as if it might heal the rift between East and West. In the event, it was a let down. The political background to the council was that the Eastern churches, Byzantium in particular, were under threat from the Islamic Ottoman Empire. The Byzantine Emperor proposed a union of East and West as the only way to prevent the collapse of Byzantium and the capture of Constantinople. The West were keen for reunification.

The Council discovered that the contentious *filioque* clause (on which, see Appendix 1) was only one of the difficulties between them. Perhaps most serious of all was the bitterness left by the fourth crusade: in 1204 the West had set out to rescue the Holy places from the Saracens in Jerusalem and yet ended up besieging and sacking Byzantium, killing many thousands of men, women, and children, fellow Christians from Constantinople, raping women (even nuns), and sacking churches, convents, and monastries, stealing the holy relics from the city. All this was rightly seen by the East as an act of unspeakable religious sacrilege. Of course, the East itself was not without sin. Western anger had been stirred by the Massacre of the Latins, a large-scale massacre of Catholics living in Constantinople in 1182. Western hostility following that atrocity lay behind the attack on Constantinople in 1203 and 1204. (It should go without saying that both of these events are utterly incompatible with the calling of the gospel-shaped church.)

However, despite their differences, all the Western and all the Eastern delegates, with the exception of two Eastern bishops (most famously Mark of Ephesus), did sign the Decree of Union on 6 July 1439. So it appeared that the schism was over.

This was not to be. When the general populous in the East, stirred by members of the Eastern Church, heard that their leaders had signed an accord with the West they almost unanimously rejected it. In our opinion this popular resistance was motivated by the bitterness left over from the atrocities committed against Constantinople by the Crusaders. Mark of Ephesus, who had refused to sign (on the grounds that he considered the *filioque* clause heretical) became a saint and those who signed the Decree of Union were reviled. (This raises an important issue—conciliar councils, ecumenical councils, and scriptural canons are all very well but you have to carry people with you.) Constantinople fell in May 1453 and after that any chance of a proper reconciliation was lost.

In recent decades there have been numerous encouraging ecumenical discussions between the Orthodox churches and the Catholic Church exploring the rocky and painful path toward the restoration of communion and unity. Pope John Paul II expressed the deep sorrow of Catholics over the thirteenth-century massacre in Contantinople to the Archbishop of Athens (2001) and to the Patriarch of Constantinople (2004). In 2004 the Patriarch formally accepted the Pope's apology in the "spirit of reconciliation of the resurrection." These are small but encouraging signs. Unity is not immanent, but neither is it unimaginable, unrealistic, or impossible.

The Second Schism: The Reformation

The second great divide in Christendom shares with the first schism the characteristic of a gradual breaking down of catholicity. While it may be true that the Roman Catholic Church maintained a powerful hegemony throughout the early Middle Ages, its influence began to wane as Renaissance humanism, the emergence of a natural philosophy that owed little to revelation, and the rise of an embryonic capitalism, weakened the omnipresent authority of the Western Church. The fact that Martin Luther nailed his famous principles of the Reformation faith to the door of the church at Wittenburg in 1517 is only an historical landmark in the greater reformation of medieval society.

Protestants like to see the Reformation as a great recovery: a return to New Testament Christianity. Undeniably, Protestantism has shown itself to be full of life and vigor, but it has also demonstrated that by its very nature it is schismatic. The Reformation became reformation *ad nauseum*, and modern denominationalism was born. This was inevitable while the reformers saw Protestantism as replacing the authority of the Pope with the authority of the Bible. It was also the case that now every person was their own "pope" and could—and did—interpret the Bible according to his or her own lights.

Furthermore, religious Protestantism paved the way for its own demise and the third schism of recent years. Once it was accepted that Scripture stood alone outside tradition, and could be interpreted correctly by anyone with a pure heart and God-given rationality (or who was led by the Spirit), it was not too big a step to suggest that the same could be said of nature. The emergence of reasoning independent from the church, begun in the Renaissance, was accelerated under Protestantism, and heralded both the rise of the scientific method and the birth of the philosophical Enlightenment of the eighteenth century. We shall explore this more in the next chapter.

With the first Great Schism, the West separated from the East; the second schism, the Reformation, saw Protestantism freeing itself from the authority of the Catholic Church. The Enlightenment, like Prometheus unbound, tore Western culture away from the authority of Christian tradition and the Bible. This not only marked the beginning of modern secularism, but it was also a key element in the slow process of the third schism.

Since that time, Protestantism has become increasingly naked and vulnerable, as its progeny (the secular doctrines of the Enlightenment) has turned on its parent with all the fury of Oedipal rage.

The Third Schism

Christianity in the Developing World, and in Eastern Europe, is clearly both growing, and often growing in a more orthodox fashion than in Western Europe and North America. It is primarily in the West that what we are calling "the third schism" has become an issue. As institutional religion has been in decline for over two hundred years, and religious categories of thought have been under constant attack for the same period, this is not very surprising. It is impossible, living in the Western world, not to be influenced by the modern worldview, and the mores and habits of the secular culture.

In the decades since the landmark publication of Bishop John A. T. Robinson's *Honest To God* (1963), the endemic nature of the third schism has become more acute; so that today we find that a significant number of ecclesiastical leaders, theologians, and many ordinary men and women, can no longer relate to the central tenets of Christianity as traditionally understood. That is to say that growing numbers of people want to remain Christian in some way, despite the fact that they can no longer assent to many of the doctrines of the creeds, believe in the Bible as a broadly reliable record of historical narratives, or find credible the possibility of miracles in either the past (including the virgin birth and resurrection of Christ) or the present. As one priest said to his congregation before they recited the Nicene Creed, "This is the part we say with our fingers crossed."

Despite the first two great schisms of Christianity, there was enough common ground to assert that there was a family resemblance of Christians, even though the family was separated and relationships impaired. This resemblance was related to a certain "orthopraxis"—a way of living and behaving that was seen as being connected in some way with an orthodoxy, a right faith or right believing. In practice the link between these two has always been tentative. It cannot be said with certainty that ordinary Christians with little theological training have always grasped the nuances, paradoxes, and presuppositions of the theologians and doctors of the church. Indeed it would probably be more accurate to assert that orthodoxy, insofar as it existed, was learned more through the medium of liturgy and rite than through sermons or formal treatise. It is an interesting point, for example, that the Eastern Orthodox often translate "orthodoxy" not as true *beliefs*, but true *worship*.

Nevertheless, however true it may be that behavior and worship tell us more of the nature of Christianity than do its beliefs taken in isolation from practice, it has always been the case that the Christian faith has been predicated upon certain beliefs that have been held to be true. Michael Goulder (1927–2010), a priest who became an atheist and resigned from holy orders, made a telling point against his friend John Hick (1922–2012), the renowned philosopher of religion. Goulder was understandably somewhat perplexed that Hick wanted to continue to call himself a "Christian" given that he no longer believed in a Holy Trinity, a literal incarnation of God-made-flesh, a bodily resurrection, or even a personal God.[1]

To put the word "Christian" in inverted commas in this way is not in order to say something unpleasant about John Hick, a man for whom we have a high regard, but is simply to register a certain awkwardness about the use of the word Christian when applied in this way. One can only

1. See Hick and Goulder, *Why Believe in God?* (1983).

9

reinterpret Christian faith so far before it ceases to be Christian faith. The atheist Professor A. J. Ayer (1910–89) similarly took issue with Professor Don Cupitt's (1934–) rather cavalier use of the word "God" in a discussion following the 1984 BBC television series, "The Sea of Faith." For Cupitt, a non-practicing Anglican priest, "God" refers not to some objective metaphysical reality external to us (a view in which God is conceived, according to Cupitt, as some cosmic tyrant) but is a product of human language, created in our image. "God" is a reality *within our language* expressing truth about *ourselves*. But, objected Ayer, God is not a word to be used in any way we please; it has a meaning that has been sanctioned by usage. Cupitt wants to retain much of the language of traditional Christianity but to reshape its meaning in ways that bear little resemblance to what Christians have always meant by such language.

It would be absurd for a member of the Communist Party to declare to his comrades that he no longer accepted the basic tenets of Marxist-Leninism but that he would stay in the Party. It would be simply odd for a Republican president to stay in office having publicly renounced free enterprise altogether. At the very least we would want to insist that, if a woman tells us that she is a radical feminist and yet believes in the desirability of patriarchy, her position is inconsistent and logically untenable.

And yet we find these not unreasonable common-sense observations are so often not applied to Christianity. This may be in part because Christians, these days, are wary of intolerance and bigotry. Heretic-hunting is unfashionable, and certainty and truth are subservient words to authenticity and tolerance. It may be that the strange language of many modern Christians who seem unable to feel at home with the old language (but do they believe in the same realities to which that language pointed?) is itself strong evidence that a major shift in consciousness has occurred.

We think that the churches are under constant pressure to undergo a revolution in thinking and perception that, far from being really new, is in fact the eventual triumph of Enlightenment consciousness over orthodox Christian thinking and experience—in practice, simply, a capitulation to the forces of critical rationalism and Romanticism. These forces have been seeking to usher in a Christianity at odds with Christian tradition for a long time now, and they have experienced some degree of success.

At times it seems that to stand on the modernist side of the divide is to see oneself as the progressive, the reformer; and the orthodox side as the counter-revolutionary, or, more appositely, the counter-reformer. From the orthodox side of the third schism, the new Christianity (though *not* the Christians who make up this new constituency) is the enemy. To stand against it is not reactionary conservativism; it is the stance of the resistance fighter defending the cause of the gospel itself.

Battle lines are by no means firmly drawn, not least because many orthodox Christians are still busy fighting the divisions of the first two schisms. Many of them do not seem to know where the new, and crucial, barricades are.

Now revisionists like Bishop John A. T. Robinson, Bishop David Jenkins, Gordon Kaufman, Maurice Wiles, John Hick, Don Cupitt, Bishop John Selby Spong, Marcus Borg, Dominic Crossan, and the like are not typical but represent in their different ways the radical extreme. But they have been influential within and without the church. And modern mass media amplifies the influence of such ideas—books by some of these thinkers become big sellers and because they are controversial and different they have an appeal to the broadcast media. The internet disseminates the thinking still further. Such thinkers offer honest and important attempts to deal with perceived conflicts between traditional Christian faith and the modern world but they do so by rejecting central elements of traditional Christian belief—Jesus as God incarnate, Jesus' resurrection and ascension, and even, in some cases, God's existence.

Now often, though not always, the radical Christians are simply trying to present the gospel in ways that connect with modern culture; to make it intelligible to modern people. We would honor their integrity, their scholarship, and much of what they have to say. All believers will agree that such projects are critical and that to do them well we need to walk that fine tightrope of listening both to contemporary culture and to the gospel. To fail to listen to our culture is to condemn ourselves to perceived irrelevance; to fail to listen to the gospel is to be in danger of simply repeating what the world is saying. Our concern in this book is that some are in danger of failing to listen to the gospel and thus of offering versions of modern Christianity which, although modern, are not Christian.

Deep Church

On 8 February 1952, C. S. Lewis wrote a letter to the *Church Times* defending the supernatural basis of the gospel, which he strongly felt was being undermined by modernism:

> To a layman, it seems obvious that what unites the Evangelical and the Anglo-Catholic against the "Liberal" or "Modernist" is something very clear and momentous, namely, the fact that both are thoroughgoing supernaturalists, who believe in the Creation, the Fall, the Incarnation, the Resurrection, the Second Coming, and the . . . Last Things. This unites them not only with one another, but also with the Christian religion as understood *ubique et ab omnibus* [lit. "everywhere and by all"]. The point of view from which this agreement seems less important than their divisions . . . is to me unintelligible. Perhaps the trouble is that as supernaturalists, whether "Low" or "High" Church, thus taken together, they lack a name. May I suggest "Deep Church"; or, if that fails in humility, Baxter's "mere Christians"?[2]

Lewis's understanding of deep church was not limited to a concept of Christian supernaturalism: the Latin tag *semper ubique et ab omnibus* (lit. that which has been believed "always, everywhere, and by all") alerts us to the fact that to talk of Christianity as it is everywhere and by everyone believed, is to appeal not only to the miraculous foundations of the Christian faith, but also to a common historical tradition of belief and practice that was normative for Christian experience. We shall explore this key idea more in this book. This championing of a common tradition was not in any sense conceived by Lewis as a "thin" or irreducible minimum of belief necessary for Christian unity. On the contrary, it was a commitment to a "thick" or maximalist form of Christianity.[3]

The most extensive definition of the common tradition of "mere Christians" given by Lewis is in his introduction to a translation of St. Athanasius's *De Incarnatione*, in which he maintains that despite the shame of a divided Christendom, the tradition has endured down the ages as solidly and as majestically as a "great level viaduct." And, he adds, it is "no insipid interdenominational transparency, but something positive and self-consistent, and inexhaustible."[4]

Lewis's description and defense of Christianity in terms of what we might call a tradition of historic orthodoxy was acknowledged by many Christians who read his works in the 1950s; but the phrase "deep church" was not adopted as a catchphrase or watchword to designate that tradition:

2. Lewis, "Mere Christians" (1952), 95.

3. By "maximalist Christianity" we mean conservative Christianity but certainly not fundamentalism. See Appendix 2.

4. Lewis, Introduction to St Athanasius, *On the Incarnation* (1944), 6–7.

the enigmatic and institutional sound of it was no match for the witty and telling pun, "mere Christianity," which soon captured the public imagination when Lewis himself chose it as the title for his edited collection of wartime broadcasting talks. Lewis, as we have seen from his letter to the *Church Times*, had commandeered the term from the Puritan divine Richard Baxter, but conceptually it was a re-imagining of the Anglican doctrine of *via media* that had originated in Richard Hooker's revisionist history of the English church in the late sixteenth century. In his seminal work, *Of the Laws of Ecclesiastical Polity* (1593), Hooker jettisoned the disjunctive view of the Protestant Reformation which stressed a radical break with the past—and thus, by implication, the notion of a common tradition—and replaced it with a history of Christian continuity that had survived the schisms of Christendom; not altogether intact or unbloodied, but nevertheless still in its essential features recognizable as the same apostolic faith of the New Testament interpreted and handed on by the fathers of the early church. The common tradition of the church for Lewis, then, pre-existed the divisions of Christendom, and, as far as he was concerned, remained the deep structure of the Christian faith.

At the outset we should say that we affirm Lewis's crucial ecumenical insight: that the divisions between Catholics and Protestants, as well as the plethora of differences among Protestant confessions, must be seen in a different light when measured against the impact of liberalism or modernism upon the church. What is at stake here is that, while we know that Jesus told his disciples that the gates of hell will not prevail against his church, the question remains as to whether we can say with any confidence that we are in the church without a knowledge of and an adherence to the common historic tradition of Christian orthodoxy. The reason it is necessary to "re-negotiate" the meaning of deep church is because more emphasis is needed than Lewis's definition allows, for the role of *liturgy* (both word and sacrament) and *spiritual disciplines* as the enabling means of grace for Christians to live in a deep church. Coming together even on the basis of a shared loyalty to the apostolic faith is not enough. And, as the charismatic renewal discovered, fellowship on the basis of shared experience is not enough either: a principled ecumenism will certainly lead to a broader church but unfortunately not necessarily a deeper one. To go all the way down, to plumb the depths of the Christian tradition, we will find that the true faith is indeed sound doctrine—"right faith"—but it is also sound action—a "rule of faith." A rule suggests right behavior, but further than that, belief and action combined finds its greatest expression in "right praise."

We must broaden (at the risk of mixing) our metaphors so that we can understand that a deep church is deep in both a solid and a liquid way. The solidity is the bedrock of faith, the dogmatic foundation of Christianity, which is Christ himself. There are also the subterranean waters and flowing streams of the Spirit. The water and the rock go together not in an accidental way but as synergy: liquid church flows to and from, in and through solid church.

To sum up an understanding of deep church, we contend that it is both a *historical* and an *existential* reality. The historical reality rests upon two givens: first, the very fact of God's self-revelation to the world in the person of his Son; and, second, the institution by the Son of his church. This historicity—of revelation and institution—has bequeathed to the people of God a living memory of what Christ has wrought on the cross for our salvation, and what he has continued to do in time through the operation of the Holy Spirit in the church (which is the main focus, though not the locus, of God's presence in the world).

It follows that this historical memory of what God has done, and continues to do, has to be accessed and cherished in order for it to become operational. We cannot be living (in) deep church if we know little or nothing about what the church has learned from experience, where and when it (or members of it) took a wrong turn, what victories it achieved, and how it learned to articulate the truths of revelation in terms of the creedal and biblical canons of the common tradition. One of the primary reasons we do not live in deep church today is because we fail to access this historical memory. Walter Brueggemann has argued that this failure is due in large part to our suffering from what he calls "gospel amnesia"—the inability to remember the principle events of salvation history.[5] More simply we might say that we have forgotten our own story. The recollecting and retelling of our story—our *anamnesia*—is to reach down to the very core of who we are as Christians so that we may recover our identity as the people of God. We cannot stress this enough; for what Christians need, to be active, faithful, and holy in our contemporary culture, is to dig down into our own deep resources.

And yet, while accessing our collective memory is a necessary feature of living fully in deep church, it is not in itself sufficient to take us and

5. Brueggemann, *Biblical Perspectives on Evangelism* (1993), esp. 90–93.

keep us there. To become part of deep church we have to experience God not only historically and intellectually but also *existentially*: when John Zizioulas wrote that the Spirit constitutes the historical church instituted by Christ,[6] he meant us to understand that this constitution of the church by the Spirit means that we as the *laos* (the people) are to be open to the presence and indwelling of the persons of the Trinity. Without the constitution of the church by the Spirit we are not ontologically a deep church but a factotum of one—a placebo effect. Church communities that have accessed the living memory of the common tradition but are not sharing in the life of the triune God are mere antiquarians rummaging around in the tradition like children looking for hidden treasures in a dusty attic. Charismatics and religious enthusiasts should take heart: deep church does not mean abandoning spiritual experience and inspirational insight for the sake of intellectual clarity and doctrinal exactitude.

Nevertheless, charismatics still face the same temptation today as they did in the 1960s: communities who are open to the presence of the Spirit (living waters) without accessing the memory of the "grand narrative" of the Christian tradition (the bedrock of faith) are liable to become fey, subject to fantasy and delusion. Perhaps tradition is not typically seen as "Spirit-breathed" (to borrow an Orthodox phrase) because it has been consigned to the status of human institution (bad/inauthentic religion), while religious experience is assigned to divine encounter (good/authentic religion).

But deep church is only truly operative when the mediated revelation of God's Son and the historical givenness of the *ekklesia* are conjoined with the immediate presence of the Spirit. In short, the institutional and the charismatic are not in opposition to each other, or in dialectical tension; they coinhere.

But deep church, while it is open to ecumenical insight and "crossover" doctrines, is not about syncretism or absorbing the next fad in the endless search for liturgical novelty. It is about the marriage between the "new thing" God is always doing in our lives, and the "old things"—the historic givens of the faith—that he has already done, which includes the means of grace that he has provided for our spiritual nourishment in the ministry of sacrament and word. Deep church, then, is not just about something old for something new. It is about *anamnesia* and acquiring the habit

---

6. Zizioulas, *Being as Communion* (1997), 123–42, esp. 132, 140.

of forgetting old slights. It is about catholicity and a holy separation. It is about a recollected history and writing a new chapter in the annals of faith.

Deep church is not merely overdue: it is an ecclesiological and missiological imperative. Mission-shaped churches and emerging churches, for all their resourcefulness, vigor, and imaginative drive, will not succeed unless they heed the lessons from their charismatic precursors in the renewal and drop anchors in the deep waters of a church that goes all the way down to the hidden reservoirs of the life-giving Spirit that, like the water that Jesus gives, gushes up like a spring to eternal life (John 4:14).

In this book we will explore further the rise of modernity and postmodernity, the cultural context in which the third schism has arisen (chapter 2). The rest of the book reflects on the notion of deep church, first through a consideration of the importance of a right understanding of the relation of Scripture and tradition (chapter 3) and then under the foci of right belief, right worship, and right action (chapters 4 to 7), before concluding with some reflections on the imperative for recovering catechesis in the contemporary West (chapter 8) and the centrality of the Eucharist (chapter 9).

2

Modernity and Postmodernity

The Roots of the Third Schism

The Rise of the Secular World

PHILOSOPHER CHARLES TAYLOR PUT the question like this: "Why was it virtually impossible not to believe in God in, say, 1500 in our Western society, while in [the twenty-first century] many of us find this not only easy, but even inescapable?"[1] Or, we might ask, how did we move from societies in which Christian faith was at the center of the way people thought about and inhabited the world to those in which it is a marginal take-it-or-leave-it hobby for those so inclined? If we are to understand the third schism we need to understand something of the rise of the modern world, the context that gave rise to the schism.

The secular realm is not some neutral space that appears once the encrusted superstition of religion is scraped away enabling people to see the world as it really is. As scholars like John Milbank, Charles Taylor, Brad Gregory, Michael Gillespie, and others have shown there is nothing inevitable or neutral about it. It is a positive social vision that has to be imagined and enacted to replace alternatives.

The tale is long and complex with many twists and turns. Much of it is a story of unintended consequences—of changes that were made for deeply religious reasons but which eventually ended up shaping the modern,

---

1. Taylor, *A Secular Age* (2007), 25.

secular world. It is a narrative both of the power of certain radical ideas to reshape the world and the power of changing patterns of social life to reshape behavior and ideas. This chapter offers merely sketches of a few important bones in the skeleton of that story. It follows a roughly chronological scheme, but be prepared for several detours and backward and forward jumps along the way.

A Medieval Debate

One bone in the skeleton is what may *seem* a rather irrelevant academic debate in the Middle Ages. However, a growing number of scholars today would see the new ideas being put forth as the root of a major change that unintentionally paved the way for the modern notion that we do not need God to make sense of the world.

The classical Christian view of God that had developed in both East and West was the long-established tradition according to which God existed on a *fundamentally different* plane of reality from creation. On this view God and creation are *radically* different. God, as the transcendent cause of all that is, is beyond human knowing. God has no *genus*—he is not one member of a certain type of being, not even the only member of that type. Indeed, God is not a being alongside others, like a human but inflated up to infinity. Rather, God is . . . *wholly other*: timeless, spaceless, bodyless, simple (meaning not composed of parts), and so on. Nevertheless, this transcendent God is immanent throughout his creation, working in and through the natural processes of the world and the events that occur. But in this way of looking at things, divine action in creation was not conceived of as simply one more cause among others. Rather, divine action was mediated through secondary causes immanent within creation—the kind of causes studied by modern sciences. God's causation operated at a *completely different level* from creational causes so there was no conflict between explaining events in terms of their primary cause (God) and secondary causes.

Now something has clearly shifted in the way that we conceive of God because in many of the contemporary debates between science and religion one of the assumptions shared by many on *both* sides is that if there is a scientific explanation for something then God did not do it. On the one hand, we find atheists claiming that science explains phenomenon X, so God is not needed to explain it. Consider Richard Dawkins's appeals to natural selection as a "blind watchmaker" replacing the need for a divine watchmaker.[2] Or consider Stephen Hawking's claims that we can explain the origins of the universe purely in terms of physical laws and we need no "supernatural being or god" to set it going.[3] On the other, we find Christians saying that phenomenon Y provides evidence for God because science cannot (possibly?) explain it. The Intelligent Design movement, for instance, takes this approach to certain features in the biological realm. Now clearly if the assumption is that scientific and theological explanations of phenomena are a zero-sum game, that one triumphs at the expense of the other, then the incredible success of the natural sciences in explaining the world around us is bound to be perceived as undermining a Christian view of the world. And if God is squeezed into the gaps in scientific explanations he becomes increasingly irrelevant for understanding the world. And this is exactly what has happened. But on the older Christian view of God such a conflict would be nonsense—scientific discoveries such as these would not undermine belief in divine actions because the cosmos was seen as sacramental, mediating divine presence.

So how did we arrive at the commonly accepted view in which Christian faith and science are seen to be in conflict? Not because of anything that science has discovered. The shift was a *philosophical* one that can ultimately be traced back to debates that occurred during the thirteenth to the fifteenth centuries. One key player was John Duns Scotus (c. 1266–1308), a Franciscan friar. He argued that although God and creatures were infinitely different they shared at least one thing in common—being, existence, reality. For Scotus, to say that a creature *exists* and to say that God *exists* is to predicate *exactly the same thing* of both. What it is for God to *be* and for a creature to *be* is the *same*, even if they are *very* different entities. God's being and that of creatures was effectively put on the same plane. The difference between us and God becomes conceived in terms of quantity—God possesses the same qualities as me *but to an infinite degree*. Another Franciscan, William of Occam (c. 1285–c. 1348), argued similarly that the word "God" denoted a discrete entity, a thing (albeit an omnipotent one), and that God was thus *a* being, the Ultimate Being, existing on the same level of reality as creation.

Two observations: first, in *no* way were these moves intended to undermine Christian faith. Their defenders were pious Christians engaged in the exercise of "faith seeking understanding." Second, the impact of these

2. Dawkins, *The Blind Watchmaker* (1986).

3. Hawking, *The Grand Design* (2010).

ideas at the time was tiny but it was a small step that turned out, in the end, to be a giant leap with large consequences. As we shall see a little later, during the scientific revolutions these ideas were picked up and, combined with certain other ideas, began to mark a road toward the expulsion of God from the cosmos. Here we simply mark the apparently innocuous shift in the way that God is conceived—relocating him on the same level of reality as creation—as the seed idea that in its full-grown forms can flower into the plant of naturalism. We shall return to this issue in due course.

The Reformation (Sixteenth Century)

In his book *The Unintended Reformation* Brad Gregory argues that the Protestant Reformation was the fundamental rupture in Western society that eventually and indirectly led to the secular world we know today. Of course, the Reformers certainly had no intentions of creating a secular society—far from it! But human actions often have long-term unpredictable consequences and so it was with the Reformation.

In the centuries prior to the Reformation there were many reform movements within the Catholic Church that were deeply pious and deeply critical of the state of the Church, seeking to reform it from within. There was a widespread awareness that European Christian society fell far short of its ideals—with corruption and sin from the peasant to the pope—and that it needed to change. What marked the Protestant Reformation apart from other reform movements was that its diagnosis of the failure of Catholic Europe was not simply that people were failing to live right but rather that the fundamental failure of the Catholic Church was its *bad doctrine*. According to Luther, Calvin, and others, the Church had departed from the teachings of the Bible and had ceased to be the true church. The solution was to recover sound doctrine and to start again outside this "whore of Babylon." To this end the Reformers turned to the Bible alone (*sola Scriptura*) as the source of Christian theology.[4] They rejected all sorts of Catholic theological claims on the grounds that they were unbiblical.

The problems with this approach quickly became clear. If the power to interpret the Bible correctly was taken out of the hands of the teaching authority of the Catholic Church, the Magisterium, and placed in the hands

4. Of course, Luther's Bible was not exactly the same as that of the rest of the church. He famously relegated some books that he did not like (such as James and Revelation) to a secondary status.

of the individual believer, then who was to decide which interpretations were right? From the 1520s multiple and inconsistent interpretations of the Bible quickly multiplied among Protestants and various rifts started to appear within the movement. Different Protestants appealed to the "clarity of Scripture" and the illumination of the Spirit in interpreting it but neither of these things stopped the multiplication of interpretations because all the Protestants involved claimed that *they* were the ones who were guided by the Spirit to understand its clear meanings.

What all sides in the theological debates of the sixteenth century—both debates between Catholics and Protestants and those between different Protestants groups—understood was that truth was at stake, that all sides could not be equally right, and that it mattered who was right. So the stakes were high yet no agreed way of resolving the differences could be found. So the more or less doctrinal uniformity of pre-Reformation Europe exploded into radical doctrinal pluralism.

Some of the Reformers—Lutherans and the Reformed—felt compelled to depend on secular authorities to promote their own versions of the faith and to defend themselves against rivals; their respective modes of Protestantism becoming the official faith of specific regions. Others (the so-called Radical Reformers) did not and found themselves at the mercy of both Catholic and Protestant states, which fought for the soul of Christendom and used force to try to put down the heretics (i.e., the other side).

To appreciate this we need to understand that religious dissent was thought to undermine the political stability of regions (the political danger of religious radicalism was believed by many to have been demonstrated by the German Peasants War of 1524–26 and the Münster affair in 1535) and so secular rulers, keen to fulfill their duty to God to promote the faith and seek the welfare of society, were willing to resist dissent. One result was that increasing amounts of state control and coercion were considered necessary to keep the lid on religious deviance with its destabilizing consequences. Another was the dependence of the churches—Catholic and Protestant—on secular authorities, authorities that over the years were to increase the limitations they placed upon religion to keep it under control. Yet another consequence was the long-lasting religious wars, including the Thirty Year War and the English Civil War, which had devastating results for European societies. And while these wars made sense from the earnest perspectives of those who fought them, their failure to achieve their goals combined with their vast economic and human costs actually worked against both Catholicism and Protestantism.

The inability to resolve the theological disputes and the huge costs of that inability had, by the seventeenth century, led to an increasing frustration among rulers and ordinary people and fueled the drive toward religious toleration, albeit limited toleration to start with. The urgent pragmatic issue became how to order society in such a way that antagonistic Christians could live together without destabilizing society. The eventual solution was the separation of religion from politics and the relegation of religious faith to the private sphere—with any and all creeds treated as equal—but the journey toward that end was gradual and winding.

The rethinking of political ideas began most obviously with Thomas Hobbes (1588–1679) and John Locke (1632–1704). Locke sought to provide a political theory that would distinguish politics and religion, state and church. The Commonwealth is simply there to procure, preserve, and advance civil interests such as "Life, Liberty, Health, and Indolence of Body; and the possession of outward things, such as Money, Lands, Houses, Furniture, and the like." Church, on the other hand, was simply "a voluntary Society of Men, joining themselves together of their own accord, in order to the publick worshiping of God, in such a manner as they judge acceptable to him, and effectual to the Salvation of their Souls."[5]

The radical thought was that states could maximize the obedience of their subjects not by enforcing religious conformity but by permitting freedom of religion. This was, after all, simply an extension of the Protestant recognition of the importance of the individual and the individual's conscience. The Dutch, although formally Reformed, promoted unheard of religious toleration (even of Catholics and Jews) in the pursuit of economic prosperity and social stability. What was pioneered in Holland was institutionalized in the eighteenth century in the United States with its formal separation of church and state. Again, we must stress that this move was not anti-religious. Most Americans at the time, and the majority even now, were religious—indeed, Christian theology was often used to justify the church/state separation and Christian values continued to undergird much of the political and social life in the USA. And the solution had much to commend it—Americans were able to work together in public life without having to agree on their Christian confessions. That's surely better than all the violence and persecution that Europe had witnessed.

5. Locke, *A Letter Concerning Toleration* (1983), 26, 28.

The potential problem was that public life was left to be shaped by the individual values of its individual citizens. That may not be a problem if most citizens happen to share moral values but what happens as common values start to fade away?

The Scientific Revolution (Sixteenth and Seventeenth Centuries)

The sixteenth and seventeenth centuries witnessed significant changes in the way in which nature and humanity's relation to it was rethought in dialogue with important scientific breakthroughs, associated with names such as Copernicus, Kepler, Galileo, and Newton.

One key element of the revolution was bracketing out of discussions Aristotle's notion of final causation, or *purpose*. Nature was examined simply in terms of efficient causation because this was much simpler to empirically test. (Although, as David Hume showed in the eighteenth century, even material efficient causation is actually impossible to demonstrate empirically. Sure, we find ourselves instinctively believing in certain circumstances that A causes B but there is no way to demonstrate that this really is the case.) So the new science set aside notions of purpose and values in nature and focused on the empirical. A divide slowly opened up between facts and values. The former was open to scientific study, the latter was not; eventually the former came to be seen as the object of knowledge, the latter the object of mere beliefs. These ideas very slowly permeated from small academic circles into popular culture.

The scientific revolution was most certainly not anti-religious. Quite the contrary, as many historians of science have shown, "theological motivations—the desire to read [God's] messages in the Book of Nature—provided the single greatest force for scientific inquiry throughout the entire early modern period."[6] Arguably, without belief in God science would never have developed. All the scientists involved were Christian believers of one sort or another (even if some, like Isaac Newton, were heterodox). They saw themselves as exploring the world that God, the Great Mathematician, had designed; thinking God's thoughts after him.

The role that science played in undermining the credibility of Christianity was indirect and gradual. It was not a result of any great clash between science and religion—as historians are well aware, new scientific discoveries

6. Principe, *The Scientific Revolution* (2011), 57.

and theories (from Copernicus to Newton to Darwin to Einstein) have generally created few significant problems for Christian theology. The so-called "war between science and religion" of popular mythology has long been exposed as a fictional retelling of history deliberately created in the late nineteenth century for ideological ends. Modern historians don't believe that myth, despite its wide currency in popular culture.

The role of science in undermining faith is much more subtle than a simple clash. It is, according to Gregory, the subtle impact on public perceptions of the greater agreement found between scientists than between religious authorities, of the clear utility of scientific results compared to the harder to quantify results of religious knowledge, of the technological solutions to practical problems that had previously driven people to prayer: "science and technology do not create atheists; they just reduce the frequency and seriousness with which people attend to religion."[7]

It is also the influence of the new mechanistic model of the universe in which the cosmos worked like a vast and complex machine—a system in which any outside influence would have to be seen as intrusions into a self-sustaining mechanism. This, when combined with the Scotist model of God as Supreme Being that we discussed earlier, made divine acts into interventions in the self-regulating, self-sustaining mechanism of the world. It also made it increasingly difficult to create any spaces for God to act in the world. He was squeezed into the gradually diminishing gaps in scientific explanations. This was part of what led to the rise of Deism, the idea that God created the universe in the beginning and then left it to run itself like a beautiful watch. God was effectively banished from acting in the world. Deism was a natural fit for the new mechanistic universe. God, in his providence, had set the world in motion and ordered it to serve the happiness of his rational creatures. Our duty to God is simply to rise to the challenge that God has set for us by using our reason to tame the world so that it serves our flourishing. Science enables us to understand how things work so that we can better manipulate them to our own ends.

However, for *some*, the application of Occam's razor (the imperative not to multiply entities more than is needed to explain a phenomenon) eventually led to the conclusion that there was no God. After all, if we can explain things scientifically, without needing to appeal to God, why even postulate God as a cause at all? And even when the growing technological consciousness does not drive people to actual atheism it can create

7. Bruce, *God is Dead* (2002), 27.

pragmatic atheists, those who may say that they believe there is a God but who, to all intents and purposes, live as if God had no bearing on their day-to-day lives. The key point to observe is that this whole logic only makes sense on the newer Scotist vision of God as an infinite being operating on the same level of reality as finite beings; acting as a cause among other causes. On the older view one would not even need to try to squeeze God into any gaps because divine causality did not operate on the same plane as creaturely causality.

The mechanistic universe changes our view of the natural world. In earlier understandings of the cosmos the realm of the senses pointed beyond itself to the transcendent, and was thus *meaning*-ful and *sign*-ificant. Beauty, truth, and goodness were part of the cosmic reality. But now the natural world becomes sharply divided from mind. Matter is just stuff that takes up space, regulates itself, and has no inherent purpose; it is not *for* something, so far as we can tell. This opens a new intellectual space in which it eventually becomes possible, although not necessary, to imagine that meaning and purpose and goodness and beauty, perhaps even truth, all exist in the realm of the intra-mental, *within us* rather than as part of the fabric of the cosmos. The mechanistic universe marks a step on the long journey to what Charles Taylor calls a "social imaginary" in which it is possible for us to locate our values, meanings, and our very *raison d'être* within ourselves. But we are jumping ahead. Let's backtrack a little.

The Enlightenment (Eighteenth Century)

The Enlightenment of the eighteenth century was born from a frustration about the inability to resolve theological disputes and the need to find a basis for exploring the world that did not depend on what were seen as arbitrary confessional foundations or claims to divine revelation. The Reformation prioritizing of the individual and its suspicion of tradition were raised to new heights and autonomous human reason was put forward as the neutral, objective, route to truth—religious and otherwise. The grand idea was that anyone who was willing to set aside prejudice, tradition, and superstition and to learn to think rationally could be led toward objective truth about the world. "The credo of modern philosophy, the various expressions of the Enlightenment, and nineteenth-century notions of progress would be that *sola ratio* could achieve what *sola scriptura* manifestly could not. A clean break with the past was necessary, rejecting Christianity's interminable doctrinal controversies and destructive religious wars."[8] Reason deserves and demands our trust and our severance from reliance on external authorities—our duty is to dare to think for ourselves.

We should not suppose that the Enlightenment was a completely antireligious movement. In France that was more the case but not in Prussia, Scotland, England, or America. Many of its key movers and players were Christians of one sort or another. They believed in their various different ways that reason and Christian faith (sometimes somewhat untraditional versions of Christian faith, of course) were compatible. But a fundamental intellectual shift had occurred in Enlightenment circles, even among those who remained Christians.

The Catholic thinker René Descartes in the seventeenth century had made *knowledge* the central issue in philosophy—what can we know and how can we know it?—and raised the bar on knowledge to unheard of heights. Against the traditional stance of intellectual inquiry as "faith seeking understanding," Descartes reversed things. He *began with doubt*, trying to doubt everything, and only granted the giddy status of "knowledge" to claims that can be *demonstrated beyond doubt*. This is a hermeneutic of suspicion rather than trust. Theology cannot meet those standards (nor, for that matter, can any area of inquiry apart perhaps from mathematics) and found itself increasingly unable to compete. Traditional Christianity was intellectually rigorous but it located rationality within the bounds of faith—one first believes in order that one may understand. The Enlightenment sought to turn things the other way around, an idea epitomized by the title of Kant's book *Religion within the Limits of Reason Alone* (1793). Religious belief was indeed permitted for Enlightenment man but it was religion *based on* and *shaped by* neutral, dispassionate reason, not tradition. This laid traditional Christian doctrines like the Trinity, the incarnation, and the resurrection open to attack. Thus one sees many who were influenced by the Enlightenment opting for Unitarianism, Deism, nonorthodox Christologies, and the like. By the end of the nineteenth century many theologians and churchmen were espousing a Jesus who was a great moral exemplar with a deep "God-consciousness," but a Jesus who looked diminishingly like the traditional Christ of the church.

8. Gregory, *The Unintended Reformation* (2012), 113.

The Rise of Capitalism and Collectivism

We need to step back for a moment to note another momentous shift in the rise of modernity: the movement to capitalist economies. A profit economy grew up in the urban markets of the medieval world, yet economics, as every other area of human life, was understood from the perspective of theology. Material things, money included, could serve the human good but could also do great harm if they became ends in themselves, acquired for their own sake. Thus in the medieval period the deadly vice of avarice was much spoken against (even if, alas, the Catholic Church did not always practice what it preached).

By the fifteenth century a profit-seeking economy with banks and imaginative new credit mechanisms was well established, influencing even the majority population in rural areas. However, the institutionalized Christian worldview did constrain the markets somewhat.

Full-blown capitalism required a radical shift in the deeply ingrained Christian condemnation of greed, which acted as a brake on the flowering of capitalism and the widespread popular acceptance that "the good life was the goods life."[9] Brad Gregory argues that it was not the economic teachings of the Catholics or the Protestants that led to this shift—*both* sides wanted to allow biblical teachings to hold back economic greed. The link between the Reformation and capitalism is more indirect—what created the conditions for the ideological shift was the *conflict* between Catholics and Protestants. As we have seen this led to the increasing separation of church and politics, and hence also economics. As things developed it became clear that the experimental Dutch Republic with its religious toleration and unembarrassed pursuit of profit was prospering while confessional states were not. By the end of the Thirty Years War and the English Civil Wars Christians across Europe were fed up with the failure of confessional states and moved toward new models that allowed for more religious toleration. Increasingly politics and economics were "liberated" from theological restraints, the utility value of items for sale was detached from their exchange value, and commerce was seen as the gateway to paradise. Religious wars became a thing of the past but wars fought for commercial gain made rational sense (as the rival Dutch and English proved in the seventeenth century). The end of that long road was the consumer society we now inhabit. Unintentionally

9. Ibid., 261.

Christians created the conditions that made *laissez-faire* capitalism a possibility and eventually a reality.

Now it is right to say that the Protestant work ethic did lend itself to material success in business. Such material blessings were often used by pious Protestant entrepreneurs for the common good but the ground was laid for those later Protestants who had the work ethic to create the wealth but not the aversion to greed found in their Reformed ancestors. Later Protestants began to identify prosperity with divine providential blessing and this too fed into the shift.

Another theological ingredient of the revolution on greed was the Protestant idea that human nature was deeply depraved and selfish. This view, once detached from a wider Christian theology, left one with a view of humans uncontrollably driven by passions seeking to satisfy their desires (so Hobbes and Hume). So it made rational sense to harness this selfishness for the good of all—avarice could actually lead toward a more healthy and happy society (so Adam Smith). It was still not celebrated as such but it was a vice that could be used for the good of all and thus encouraged as a lesser evil. And there can be no doubt that capitalism, despite its many problems, has indeed raised standards of living for many, many people.

We ought to mention as a brief coda to this section that capitalism was not the only form of economic organization that has characterized modernity. The nineteenth century witnessed a backlash against capitalism and the development of a very different but *equally modern* political and economic model—Marxist communism. Communism as worked out in the Soviet block was just as committed to rational economics, scientism, and industrial development as Western capitalism. What differentiated communism from its nemesis was its collectivist and state-controlled approach, as opposed to the individualist and market-driven orientation of capitalism. Communism was a force to be reckoned with throughout the twentieth century but, while it still exerts influence, the collapse of the USSR vastly diminished its appeal and power. Even communist China is now very capitalist in its peculiar mode of communism.

The Industrial Revolution (Nineteenth Century) and the Consumer Age

The Rise of Consumerism

Modernity was born, and the ideas of the Enlightenment became the stuff of everyday life. In themselves the doctrines of the eighteenth-century philosophers carried conviction but lacked potency. The massive social upheavals of the nineteenth century, with the move from the country to the towns, the explosion of cities, the dazzling success of science and technology, and the growth of industrialism and bureaucracy, provided the muscles and sinews that enabled the Enlightenment to come fully to life: it insinuated itself into the consciousness of Victorian men and women, found its way into the language and syntax of both specialist and mundane speech, and created a new culture.

The technological developments during the Industrial Revolution, motivated by growing consumption, vastly accelerated the rise of capitalism by making more goods available to domestic markets at cheaper and cheaper prices.

In the eighteenth century the consumption of "luxuries" was restricted to the aristocracy. The new mechanical mass production methods of the nineteenth century changed that by making products more affordable. But the markets were determined by government and industry rather than by the public at large. After the austerity years of World War II there was full employment and a rising standard of living and entrepreneurs realized the potential of the new markets. They used industrial methods to create consumer durables for the public at large, and thus was born our age—the age of consumerism.

It was an age built on the selling of lifestyle dreams with goods that were designed to become obsolete and to be replaced by a never-ending flow of new products. The technologically-enabled mass media—magazines, radio, television, and later the internet—all played their role in stoking the fires of consumer desire through relentless advertising, the creation of celebrities to aspire to, and beatific visions of the goods life. Desires become needs in the advertisers' crucible, a route to the happiness and fulfillment that we all deserve—because we're worth it. Our identity becomes defined and constantly redefined by what we wear, what we own, where we live, what we drive, where we eat—"I shop, therefore I am."

Consumerism is insatiable—it survives by promising heaven and then delivering Milton Keynes. So long as each new product is one step closer to "heaven" consumers will keep buying, seeking their "heavenly ascent," and the system is fed for another day.

Consumerism is amoral—it does not aspire to good or evil—all it cares about is feeding . . . and it is very, very hungry. It will sell what people desire and it will stoke whatever desires it needs to in order to sell (so long as it does not break any laws, and even then . . .). If those desires are good and healthy then the markets will provide good and healthy products; if they are bad and degrading then the markets will provide products to fit. The consumer is king (even if s/he needs a little manipulating en route).

Scientism and Romanticism

Backtracking from modern consumerism to the nineteenth century again we need to explore the rise of scientism. One of the consequences of the vast multiplication of inconsistent Christian truth claims and the inability to resolve them was a growing cynicism in elite society about all such claims. Religion increasingly appeared just subjective and literally arbitrary (i.e., simply a function of the human will) and unable to get us to objective truth. This contrasts with the sciences, which had shown themselves to be very successful in generating broad consensus across ideological and cultural divides. Victorians, including the young John Stuart Mill, were so overcome by the success of the physical sciences that many believed with Auguste Comte (1798–1857), the father of sociology, that it was only a matter of time before morality and religion would be explained by science. This optimism gave rise to scientism: a doctrine that insisted that all reality and truth were now circumscribed by science. Indeed, for Comte, the young Mill, Herbert Spencer, and to a certain extent the mature Karl Marx, science took on the character of true knowledge, while religion was reduced to mere opinion.

C. S. Lewis was right when he asserted that Darwinism subsequently provided the scientific underpinning for the progressive idealism of Kant's rationality. Once it was believed that progress had a scientific basis, this spilled over into another ideology: Darwinism-as-a-worldview; that is, a version of Darwinism that no longer saw itself as just a biological theorem but as a principle of progress in the universe itself. This worldview-Darwinism is found in various forms in Marx, Spencer, and Fabianism, and was later to spawn twentieth-century Fascism and the eugenics used in Nazi Germany.

During the nineteenth century there was a Romantic backlash against the arid certainties of positivism and scientism. Romanticism is notoriously difficult to define but can be roughly thought of as a European cultural movement that

> privileged the imagination as a faculty higher and more inclusive than reason, which sought solace in or reconciliation with the natural world, which "detranscendentalized" religion by taking God or the divine as inherent in nature or in the soul and replaced theological doctrine with metaphor and feeling, which honored poetry and all the arts as the highest human creations, and which rebelled against the established canons of neoclassical aesthetics and against both aristocratic and bourgeois social and political norms in favor of values more individual, inward, and emotional.[10]

When one thinks of romanticism one thinks of poets (like Novalis, Byron, Wordsworth, Coleridge, Shelley, and Keats), novelists (like Hugo, Goethe, Walter Scott, and Mary Shelley), artists (like Turner, Constable, Blake, and Goya), musicians (like Beethoven, Schubert, Berlioz, Strauss, Mendelssohn, Chopin, and Wagner), and philosophers (like Rousseau, Fichte, Schiller, and Schelling)—people whose names are still widely known and whose influence still reverberates through Western cultures.

Protestantism partly embraced positivism, and partly tried to disengage itself. Two theological trends stand out as markers toward the third schism.

Right at the beginning of the nineteenth century, Friedrich Schleiermacher (1768–1834), "the father of modern theology," convinced that Kant had proved the impossibility of approaching God through rationalistic philosophy, and anxious to avoid both sterile rationalism and dogmatic revelation, opted for *experience* as the touchstone of certainty in faith. His was a Christianity influenced by the Romantic sensibility.

Schleiermacher's influence on Protestant theology has been colossal, and is directly linked with sophisticated and ingenious interpretations of Scripture. Albert Ritschl (1822–89), another exceptionally influential German theologian, saw himself as developing Schleiermacher's project: faith, he said, was grounded in the religious experience and value judgments of

10. Ferber, *Romanticism* (2010), 10–11.

31

the religious community rather than in facts. As such it is beyond the scope of reason.

This Romantic emphasis on authentic faith (the first theological trend) sought to insulate Christianity from the impact of the growing historical criticism of the Bible (the second theological trend). Since the Jewish philosopher Benedict Spinoza (1632–77) had interpreted the Bible with unprecedented historical skepticism an increasing number of biblical scholars, especially in Germany, began to look at the Scriptures not as sacred canon, but as scientific object. They felt that they wanted to go beyond the overlay of theological understanding imposed on the Bible to the primary data of the historical Israel, the historical Jesus, and the historical church. And the "real" history they thought they found behind the veil of the texts looked less and less like the story believed in by the church. The Romantic move made by many theologians was in part an attempt to retain the validity of faith in the face of the application of scientific approaches to the Christian Scriptures. And it allowed theologians to reject or reinterpret quite a lot of traditional Christian beliefs while feeling that the faith itself was not threatened in the process. As such many of the theologians who embraced the first trend (Romanticism) *also* embraced the second ("scientific" study of the Bible).

But the quest(s) for the historical Jesus led to a wedge being driven between the Christ of faith and the first-century Jew from Palestine. Since that time, modern theology has sometimes oscillated between a view of Christ as almost all Spirit, bereft of the humanness of Jesus, or as a mere historical figure empty of divineness.

Secularization

It is time to shift gear and to take a look back at the big picture through the work of some sociologists. Our focus will be on the trajectory of secularization. We need to be careful not to confuse secularization with secularism. Secularization is the complex of social processes by which religious thinking, practices, and institutions become socially marginalized. Secularism, on the other hand, is an ideological and political program that sets out to actively achieve a strict separation of state and religious institutions and to ensure that all religious and non-religious beliefs are equal before the law. Our focus here is on secularization and not secular*ism*.

The loss of social significance for Western Christianity, most especially European Christianity, is the result of a long and complex interaction of new ideas and social processes.

Industrialization led to urbanization, which in turn led to specialization of roles and institutions and a growth of sub-cultures and pluralism. This increasingly complex society required more overarching organization: life became organized at the level of the nation state rather than at the local level (what sociologists call societalization) and in increasingly bureaucratic ways, as opposed to the face-to-face relationships of rural communities.

The new factories needed workers and life in the countryside was hard, so there was a great migration as people looked for work in cities. The vast move of populations into cities during the nineteenth and twentieth centuries, and continuing today, has had huge implications. Religion functions well in small, stable, rural communities in which everyone knows everyone and everyone has a role. Religion could give expression to the shared values and beliefs of small and medium-sized communities.

> The church of the Middle Ages baptized, christened and confirmed children, married young adults, and buried the dead. Its calendar of services mapped onto the temporal order of the seasons. It celebrated and legitimized local life. In turn, it drew considerable plausibility from being frequently reaffirmed through the participation of the local community in its activities. In 1898 almost the entire population of my local village celebrated the successful end of the harvest by bringing tokens of their produce into the church . . . [T]he church provided a religious interpretation of an event of vital significance to the entire community . . . When the total, all-embracing community of like-situated people gives way to the dormitory town or suburb, there is little held in common to celebrate.[11]

Urbanization leads to the break-up of such communities and the boundaries of social control that shape the belief and behavior of individuals within them. The anonymity of the city forms a context in which the individual is much freer to attend or not attend church, for instance. But the diversity of the city also offers the individual inhabitant a wide range of alternatives to church. Of course, the disorientation of such a context for some people will push them into churches, where they can find friendship with like-minded people (witness the size of first-generation immigrant

11. Bruce, *God is Dead* (2002), 13.

churches), but it can just as easily lead to people falling away from church involvement. There are so many alternatives to church in the city and who will know if I don't get involved?

The size and complexity of cities led to growing *institutional differentiation*. We tend to think of churches as focused on religious worship but it used to be the case that a wide range of social roles were fulfilled by churches. They were not simply providers of religious services but also of health care, education, social work, entertainment, as well as all the life cycle events from birth, through marriage, to burial. The process of modernization has led to the setting up of a vast range of specialist organizations to take over these important responsibilities. One negative consequence of this for churches is that their perceived social significance can be very much reduced. Churches now just do "religious stuff" and if that's not your thing then they have no relevance. And even if it is your thing the churches' relevance can still be greatly reduced. The heart of the secularization thesis is not so much that religious belief and practice disappear but their *significance* in the social system diminishes as a result of the processes of modernization. (Though, as José Casanova has shown, the differentiation of social roles at the heart of modernity does not *have* to mean that religion departs from the public sphere.[12])

Various factors from the seventeenth through twentieth centuries led to a *split between public and private worlds*. The public world is the world of government, of business, of work, of the economy, of education, of health, of scientific research, of the police and army. The private world, on the other hand, is the world of family and voluntary organizations. It is where we relax and can believe and feel and act as we wish (so long as we do not infringe the rights of others to believe and feel and act as they wish). The public world came to be dominated by pragmatic, instrumental reason that aims at maximizing efficiency by tailoring means to ends. By contrast, the private world is the world of emotional escape from the harsh impersonal and rationalistic realm of the public sphere—the Englishman's home is his castle.

Individuals inhabit both worlds but they need to act and speak in ways appropriate to the different spheres. All sorts of behaviors that are fine in the private sphere may be considered unprofessional or inappropriate in the public sphere. This way of dividing up the world was unknown before modernity but seems second nature now. Of course, the barrier between

12. Casanova, *Public Religions in the Modern World* (1994).

the two spheres is not at all solid, indeed it can be quite porous, and many tensions are generated in the cross-pollination. It may even be that the line between the spheres is becoming increasingly porous as we move beyond modernity.

In the past Christianity profoundly influenced politics, law, education (from the school to the university), economics, welfare, and healthcare. As we have seen, many of the public social roles were taken over from churches by the state as part of the modernization process and church was increasingly relegated to the private sphere. So churches occupy a slot in the modern world as one voluntary organization alongside other such organizations (chess clubs, book reading clubs, charities, and the like)— something to opt into in one's leisure time if one feels so inclined. This new location for religion on people's mental map of the world, of course, can have the effect of undermining the importance of church.

The growth of cities also leads to *the pluralization of beliefs*, a trend magnified by the far greater awareness of other cultures and beliefs that has resulted from increased immigration, the cheap availability of overseas travel, and the ability of modern media to bring the world to our living rooms. Sociologist Peter Berger explains how the increasing pluralization of beliefs impacts religious believers psychologically. In Christendom religious faith was just *a given*. Rejecting God's existence, say, was the psychological equivalent of a modern person not believing in planets other than earth. The world is not like that now. Modern people cannot but be aware of the vast range of religious beliefs out there to choose from. *At the very least* this has the psychological effect of making modern religious believers less certain of their beliefs than premodern generations would have been. As Steve Bruce comments, "When the oracle speaks with a single clear voice, it is easy to believe it is the voice of God. When it speaks with twenty different voices, it is tempting to look behind the screen."[13] Berger maintains that the psychological plausibility of beliefs is reinforced or undermined by social structures, what he calls "plausibility structures."[14] Thus, if certain beliefs are reinforced in our family, in church, in school, at work, on TV, in the newspapers, by scientists, in politics, and so on, we will find it very plausible. However, to the degree that beliefs lack such reinforcement they lose credibility and become increasingly uncertain. In the premodern European world Christian faith was deeply reinforced by all the relevant

13. Bruce, *God is Dead* (2002), 18.
14. Berger, *The Heretical Imperative* (1980).

social structures. It was simply beyond reasonable doubt. But the "sacred canopy"[15] of this overarching religious worldview has been broken. The modern state, unlike the rulers of Christendom, does not see its role as that of serving God's kingdom and working alongside his church but as that of guarding fair competition between competing religious and non-religious groups and this encourages a resistance to reinforcing particular religious beliefs in the public square.

The religious and ethical hyperpluralism of the modern world undermines our psychological certainty in our beliefs. And with the evacuation of religion from the public realm a modern Westerner can go to school, watch television, read books, go shopping, play sports, engage politically, go to hospital, do science, and live their entire lives without any direct reinforcement of the faith in God that they would find in a church. What *is* socially reinforced, even if unintentionally, is that God is at best marginally relevant and this implicit message impacts even Christian believers. So it is little wonder that for many Western people it feels like the world seems to get by very well without God; that Christianity is not relevant to their lives; that belief in God seems to be equivalent to belief in Santa Claus; that belief in Christ seems to be no more than an optional extra, a hobby. It is little wonder that Christians themselves sometimes struggle with doubt. And often this is not doubt brought on by significant intellectual challenges to Christian faith but simply doubt brought on by the lack of reinforcement from plausibility structures in the worlds we inhabit. As Duncan MacLaren notes, "Christianity is far less credible today than its credentials deserve."[16] It is not simply that people do not go to church because they do not believe. It is just as true that people do not believe because they do not go to church. And it is not so much that modern people *reject* Christianity as that they are utterly *indifferent* to it.

But if pluralism has been present in a culture from the outset the story can be different. Here we need to be aware of important differences between Europe and America and indeed within Europe itself. David Martin argues that the impact of modernization on Christianity depends on where a country is starting from in terms of church-state links. Catholic countries in Europe with strong state-church relations remained very resistant to modernization, allowing little religious dissent. This led to more extreme tensions with the forces of modernization, forces that felt compelled to

15. Berger, *The Sacred Canopy* (1967).
16. MacLaren, *Mission Implausible* (2012), 95–96.

resist both state *and church* (as seen in the French Revolution and the Spanish Civil War). As a consequence both France and Spain are now deeply secular with a lot of residual anti-Christian sentiment. (There were exceptions to this pattern, such as Poland because the Catholic Church there was seen as the national force of resistance against an unwanted Communist state.) In Protestant countries with a state church, such as Great Britain, there was more toleration of religious dissent. Thus modernizing tendencies could oppose the state church, the Church of England, without feeling that they were opposing *Christianity itself.* Indeed, much of the drive toward modernization came from non-conformist Christians (Baptists, Presbyterians, Congregationalists) with their vision of a "free church and a free state." Thus the drive toward modernization did generate some resentment against Christianity but not as much as in some Catholic countries. Countries, such as the USA, in which pluralism and religious freedom were the norm from the start, could experience political revolution without churches being resisted at all. And religious participation in the USA is far higher than anywhere in Europe in spite of the fact that the USA is a modern, urbanized, nation in which religion is privatized and religious pluralism is endemic.[17] "The American pattern of privatizing religion while at the same time allowing it some public functions has proven highly compatible with the religious pluralism that has characterized America from the colonial period and grown more and more pronounced."[18] Martin's point was that "religion flourished most luxuriantly under modern conditions where church and state were separated and where there was religious pluralism and competition."[19]

Secularization was by no means inevitable—it is not a necessary consequence of economic, political, and intellectual development; history did not *have* to unravel the way that it did. But it did. Nor is it the end of religion. Religion can thrive in the secular city (as is seen most clearly outside Europe, in the USA, in which church practice rose steadily from 1800 to 1950,[20] in Asia, Africa, and Latin America) and there are even significant

---

17. Martin, *A General Theory of Secularization* (1978).

18. Bellah, *Habits of the Heart* (1985), 225.

19. Martin, "Sociology, Religion, and Secularization" in *On Secularization* (2005), 21.

20. Though we should note that in recent years the general trend in the USA seems to be toward gradual decline in religious participation (along with participation in all sorts of social activities). See Putnam, *Bowling Alone* (2001), esp. chap. 4.

pockets of desecularization that one can see across Europe.[21] One must be wary of making Europe the paradigm that the rest of the world will follow.

Where Are We Now?

Modernity simply refers to the modern era in Western cultures, from the sixteenth century onwards—a period of profound economic, technological, social, intellectual, and political change, as described above. Modern*ism*, on the other hand, may best be thought of as a broad term indicating an *intellectual and aesthetic orientation* marked by the trust in reason and science and the suspicion of tradition that increasingly characterized modernity.[22] The controversial question is whether Western cultures are still in modernity or whether they have moved or are moving into a new era of *post*-modernity marked by an intellectual and aesthetic orientation that could be described as postmodernism.[23]

There is much discussion as to how best to interpret the changes in contemporary Western cultures. What all commentators seem to agree on is that classical modernity has changed since the rise of consumerism in the 1950s. It is helpful to get some sense of the *continuities* and *discontinuities* between modernity and the emerging cultural context, whether we call it post-, late-, or ultra-modernity.

Late Modernity

In terms of key elements of modernity in its differing forms, much remains firmly entrenched, albeit in evolving forms:

Capitalist economies. Capitalism in the West has changed as societies have moved from industrial to post-industrial economies. But capitalism is far more, not less, entrenched than ever. Indeed, with the collapse of modernity's alternative economic system—communism—and the rise of global capitalism there is little likelihood of this changing (in spite of growing public disquiet about the dark underbelly and inequalities of global capitalism and the periodic economic collapse). Indeed, the functional

21. See Davie, *Religion in Modern Europe* (2000); MacLaren, *Mission Implausible* (2012), chap. 4.

22. Modernism is often used to describe a movement in the Arts between the 1850s and the 1950s but we are using the term more broadly.

23. We should stress that we are speaking of *Western* cultures here.

rationality of economic models is increasingly being taken as the paradigm for *all* areas of public life with the goal of enabling the maximal outputs in healthcare, education, policing, and so on. Every good has to be quantifiable and commensurable so that we can make rational decisions on how to proceed—how to get the most bang for the bucks we invest in hospitals, schools, art galleries, police forces, and the like.

Urbanization. The process of urbanization that was greatly accelerated during the Industrial Revolution continues unabated. In 1800 only 3 percent of the world's population lived in cities; by 2008 that number had risen to 74 percent in the developed world and 44 percent in the developing world. By 2050 the urban population is expected to rise to 70 percent of the world's population. However, what has changed is that urbanization's role as the key means of furthering modernization has been supplemented by, perhaps even usurped by, the rise of mass media technologies.

Societalization. The organization of society at national and regional rather than local levels, remains in place. Indeed, increasingly we are seeing societalization at an *international* level with international trade agreements, international courts of human rights, international businesses. This trend, alongside deregulated global markets and growing global online communities are decreasing the role of the nation state. The top-down organization of modernity is now complicated by the bottom-up influences unleashed most especially by the internet. Now anyone with a computer can seek to exert an influence through websites, blogs, YouTube, Facebook, Twitter, and the like. They can make their own views, music, movies, photographs, or whatever available to the world.

Differentiation of social roles so that the roles of churches are increasingly limited to "religious" stuff remains a feature of contemporary Western societies (although the picture is varied and complex across Europe and America).

Privatization of religion. The place of religion in the public sphere of the modern world has varied a lot in different nations in different times. But as explained above the trend has been toward minimizing or even excluding it from the public world. This remains the case and indeed there are increasingly vocal ideological secularists who are pushing to enforce the *complete expulsion* of religion from the public realm. Traditional religion often resists this relegation, most especially Islam, which simply *cannot* recast itself as a non-political religion without betraying its very heart. But Christians too have been active in the public realm. Consider the rise of the religious right in America. Even though church and state are kept separate by law very many American Christians still work to bring what they see as Christian values to bear on national public life. Christianity (of a certain variety) remains a very potent force in American politics.

The centrality of the individual and the rights of the individual. This key theme of the Reformation, reconfigured in the Enlightenment, has become more and more fundamental in the consumerist world of the modern West. The individual is at the center. But there have been changes here too. With the growth of the consumer society there has been a growing shift toward the individual reconceived as the *hedonistic* individual—s/he who has the right to maximize her/his own pleasures. And with the increasing mobility of the population and the consequent impermanence of local communities individuals find themselves more and more alone. The phenomenal growth of online communities and social networks serves as a superficial substitute for community but the individual retains the power to opt in and out of such relationships in ways impossible in embodied relationships. This leads to a generation that longs for deep community but increasingly can only handle fleeting and ever-shifting superficial communities.

Of course, the individual has morphed somewhat. The postmodern individual has been subjected to de-centering and deconstructing. This self is not "given" but must be constructed and deconstructed and reconstructed as it sees fit. People are more proactive in managing their image than ever before—electronically enhancing photographs, carefully crafting online social network profiles and self-presentations, even modification of their bodies through diet, fitness, tattoos, piercing, and plastic surgery. It is all "surface" stuff but there is an increasingly sense that the surface stuff is all there is to the self, or, at least, all that matters.

Science. The high respect for science as a means of knowing about reality and manipulating it for our benefit remains in place—indeed societies are more dependent than ever on technology; just imagine the *enormous* impact of a total loss of electricity for one week. We show our trust in science by the way that we trust our very lives to it every day. At the same time there has been a growing tension in the popular view of science. There is unease created by the realization that scientists disagree on certain issues and change their minds on certain issues; that science, in other words, can get things wrong. There has also been a growing realization that scientists can be influenced by ideology, ambition, commercial and political pressure, and that this too casts a shadow over the reliability of the results. So while science is still held in high regard, that regard is more tentative than in previous generations.

We should also note that the success of the sciences is in part a result of their deliberate restriction of their field of inquiry to bracket out fundamental questions of meaning, purpose, values, and metaphysics. But people still want to know about those big questions and increasingly realize that science will not provide the answers. This leads postmodern people to reject the scientism of the nineteenth century and the first half of the twentieth century and to be more open to truth of some kind beyond the scope of science.

In general terms, in all these areas the worlds we live in remain very much in continuity with modernity, albeit with some developments.

Postmodernity

Some of the cultural changes that the Western world is experiencing really do seem to be a move beyond modernity and can be aptly described as "*post*modern." At the level of ideas one major change has been the growing loss of confidence in the power of reason. We could say that post/late modernity is modernity with an epistemological headache. The idea that autonomous reason was neutral and objective and could guide unprejudiced thinkers to see the world as it really is has been subject to a whole host of critiques. There is a much greater awareness that all thinking is located and non-neutral. And this loss of confidence is not simply in the academy but is widely disseminated in the general population. In particular, when it comes to matters that science cannot settle—religious beliefs, ethical beliefs, beliefs in life after death, and so on—there is a very widely shared belief that reason cannot discover the truth. One must simply make a blind leap of faith. This is different from modernity. There, although it was generally recognized that religious and ethical disputes could not be settled by appeals to authorities that were not shared (e.g., tradition, the Bible), there was still a belief that *reason* could guide us toward truth. That expectation is now much diminished because the convergence on shared truth promised by the Enlightenment concept of reason did not happen. As any study of modern philosophy from Descartes to Derrida would reveal, there is as much agreement between philosophers about any given subject (e.g., ethics, epistemology, aesthetics, metaphysics, language, mind) as there is between interpreters of the Bible. The hyperpluralism of truth claims has not been tamed by the power of reason.

In modernity, even when people tolerated their differences in religious belief there was still generally a shared understanding that conflicting claims could not all be true. I may have been happy to live alongside my Catholic neighbor but I still thought that he was mistaken in his beliefs. In post/late modernity one is more likely to come across the idea that nobody is right or wrong on such questions. Religious "truth" there may be but it is person-relative—the autonomous individual decides on their own truth. No one else should presume to sit in judgment on such personal decisions. And each individual has the right to make such decisions. The value of religion is in its therapeutic power—if people find it helpful, who are we to say it's wrong? This is, as Gregory puts it, "religion of the individual, by the individual, and for the individual."[24] Or, in the words of the Manic Street Preaches, "This is my truth, show me yours."

Ultra Modernity

As an example of how the new cultural context in the West exaggerates aspects of modernity, and can aptly be described as *ultra* modernity, consider the omnipresence of consumption. As standards of living rose and people's expectations of the material quality of their lives has risen and risen, the pursuit of consumer goods has become the passion of our age. And it is a time-consuming passion. Indeed the consumer mentality has arguably become the dominant mindset in the way we approach many areas of life. People work hard to earn the money to spend on their enjoyment, and religious commitment has suffered as a result. This truly is ultra modernity.

The consumer mindset has come to dominate the way we approach many aspects of life—the consumer rules, not just when we shop for goods but also increasingly in our interactions with schools, hospitals, and churches. We hunt down whatever satisfies our needs and if we feel that it is not doing so we move elsewhere. Customer loyalty is almost a thing of the past—we feel no obligation to continue a relationship unless we continue to benefit from it.

> What until moderately recently was simply imposed . . . or inherited . . . becomes instead a matter of personal inclination. I go to

24. Gregory, *The Unintended Reformation* (2012), 171.

church (or to another religious organization) because I want to, maybe for a short period or maybe for longer, to fulfill a particular rather than a general need in my life and where I will continue my attachment so long as it provides what I want, but I have no obligation either to attend in the first place or to continue if I don't want to.[25]

This puts churches in the position of having to compete for customers and to keep them happy or lose them.

Post Modernity as an Opportunity to Recover Deep Church

Christendom is gone forever and there is no point in wishing it would come back. The Christendom model can only work, as far as any political model works (i.e., imperfectly), in certain kinds of society, but such societies no longer exist and will not do so again. The church is called to get on with being the people of God rather than wishing things had turned out differently.

This chapter has sought to sketch the rise of the cultural context in which the Western church must be church. That context has brought unprecedented challenges—after all, modernity created the conditions that gave rise to the third schism within the church and those conditions remain with us to quite some extent. Nevertheless, the epistemological crisis within modernity has opened a space within which Christian theology can cease bowing before the monolithic notion of universal reason. The idea that standards internal to scientific rationality should be the standard for *all* truth-seeking is now a highly contested notion rather than "given." As John Milbank says, theology "no longer has to measure up to the accepted secular standards of scientific truth or normative rationality."[26] This creates space for Christian theology to be true to itself.

What C. S. Lewis called "chronological snobbery," the notion that newer ideas are always better then older ones, is also no longer assumed. There is a growing openness to learning from "the wisdom of the ancients." Tradition is no longer treated with automatic suspicion, though it has not and will not recover the automatic trust it had in pre-Reformation times. Thus theology is now able "to make a kind of half-turn back to pre-modernity"[27]

25. Davie, *The Sociology of Religion* (2007), 96.

26. Milbank, "Postmodern Critical Augustinianism" (2009), 49.

27. Ibid.

But only a half-turn. Christians *cannot* think and behave as if modernity has not happened. And going back has to be a post-critical retrieval in full awareness of what has transpired in between. And it cannot be with the aim of simply *repeating* the theology and practice of past Christianity. Rather, it must be a retrieval that has an eye to recontextualizing in our living contexts—a fresh improvisation of the faith that is both deeply rooted in Scripture and tradition but also alive to the worlds we now inhabit. Christian tradition has never been a static notion. As Paul Ricoeur pointed out, living traditions are dynamic and contain an element of both sedimentation and innovation. Living traditions move into the future by remembering their past (the sediment of the tradition) and developing in continuity with it (innovating within the tradition).[28] We could describe this as "remembering our future." Or we could call it "deep church." It is our contention in this book that the only way in which the church can survive the wound of the third schism and navigate the rapids of modernity and postmodernity is by *anamnesis*, by remembering, by recovering deep church.

Before we consider the *orthodoxia* and *orthopraxia* essential to deep church we need to better appreciate the classical Christian approach to the authority of Scripture and tradition. To this we turn in the next chapter.

28. Ricoeur, *Time and Narrative* (1984), 68–70.

PART TWO

Deep Church:
On Recovering the Gospel

3

Deep Roots

On Relating Scripture and Tradition

Introduction: On Losing Our Memories

"The smartphone has become the sacrament (James K. A. Smith calls it the 'liturgical instrument') of the postmodern city," writes blogger Matthew Tan.[1] All the forces of contemporary urban life embrace each other at that mobile "holy" site. "One thing that the smartphone demonstrates about the contemporary city," he continues, "it is that our social context is hostile to memory. Indeed, the postmodern city is proactively destructive of memory." Consider the way that emails—disposable communications—quickly disappear out of sight and out of mind. The smartphone is focused on *the now*. "The city embodies a culture of authenticity that emphasises living in the now. 'Now' is the special messianic moment within postmodern culture. However, this . . . 'now' is deliberately cut off from its connections with the past as well as the future, and life for the urban dweller ends up becoming a process of disjointed present moments." By breaking time up into "manageable micro-units" we are liberated from being determined by our past. And the postmodern city can fill our presents with a never-ending supply of pleasures to "take our mind off things."

But memory cannot be cast aside so easily. Indeed, for Christians memory *must not* be cast aside. We can only live a flourishing life in the

1. Matthew Tan, "Smartphones, Memory, and the Cross," http://divinewedgie. blogspot.com.au/2012/10/smartphones-memory-and-cross.html. All subsequent quotations are from the same blog post.

now if we know who we are, and to know who we are we need to remember where we have come from and where we are going. This Christian identity-forming memory is preserved in Scripture and tradition and passed on from generation to generation. But since the Reformation, and especially since the Enlightenment, tradition has come under attack. But while some may see tradition as a liability for the church in the modern West, locking us into permanent irrelevance, we shall suggest that the future of the church in the West depends upon our rooting ourselves in the tradition. If we lose our memories we lose our identity and instead of being a counter-cultural gospel people we become mere religiously tinted mirrors of the world around us.

The eighteenth-century Enlightenment was a cultural movement that sought to liberate humanity from "enslavement" to tradition, calling people to think for themselves. "*Enlightenment is man's emergence from his self-incurred immaturity*," wrote Kant. "*Sapere aude!* Have courage to use your own understanding!"[2] Reason, not tradition, was the source of authority for "modern man."

This suspicion of tradition, this lovechild of the Reformation, resonated with those already suspicious of Roman Catholicism and found a natural home in some Protestant contexts (and in Revolutionary France). But, of course, it was a dangerous child for it cast its eye of suspicion not merely upon the Christian tradition but also upon the Bible itself. That suspicion of Scripture was something much more troubling for good Protestants.

This is not the context to explore the diverse and complex ways that different Christians in Europe and America tried to navigate the new enlightened world. But we do need to examine afresh the place of tradition in Christianity. Our contention is that the authority of tradition is an *essential* component of Christian faith and that any attempts to contextualize the faith in the modern West must resist the temptation to make it "relevant" by jettisoning the claims of the tradition. That route is a wide road that leads to destruction.

It is also our contention that an appreciation of the authority of tradition will reveal its symbiotic relationship with Scripture. Rather than undermining the authority of the Bible, as some evangelicals have worried, Scripture and tradition belong together like a team in a three-legged race.

One of the benefits of the postmodern shift is that there is a fresh appreciation of the ubiquity of tradition and the myth of neutral rationality.

2. Kant, "What is Enlightenment?" (1996), 51.

This has opened up space for Christians to explore the great tradition again without the embarrassment of seeming irrational or backwards. Indeed, there is a wind of change blowing even through the evangelical world, carrying on its wings a new watchword, which is neither "renewal" nor "revival," but *retrieval*. What is new about this retrieval is that it is a quest for something old, and its modus operandi is not a technique, but a turning back (*epistrophe*).

Tradition and Traditions

This modus operandi, this act of turning, is what C. S. Lewis calls a "regress"; not in the modern sense that we are retrogressing or degenerating, but in the Latin sense of *regressus*—of returning or going back to a former place. The purpose of going back is not one of antiquarian curiosity, but to retrieve something that we have lost in order to make the church vital again in the present. And the something that evangelicals and others have lost and need to retrieve is *tradition*.

To be sure, most of us are happy with and pride ourselves on our own denominational traditions or customs—those things that mark us off and delineate us from each other. But the above mentioned retrieval is not concerned with traditions such as these. Rather it is concerned with the *paradosis* of the church—that which in times past was believed to be the apostolic tradition of the New Testament, and which was handed on and jealously guarded by the community of faith. These days, however, *paradosis* is almost exclusively defined in most theological dictionaries as the actual process of handing on or handing over the faith, rather than as a substantial, albeit static, body of doctrines and practices or a fixed apostolic deposit of faith. However, *paradosis* in Scripture and for the fathers is as much concerned with that which is handed on—the *content* of tradition— as it is with its *transmission* across the generations and down the ages.

Fr. Georges Florovsky and Vladimir Lossky, the prominent Orthodox theologians of the Russian Diaspora, cross the boundaries of understanding *paradosis* as either static content or dynamic process, by describing tradition as a living reality infused with the Holy Spirit and encountered through worship, rather than restricting it to an official list of approved doctrines by the church authorities.[3] Bishop Kallistos calls this approach

3. For Lossky, "Tradition, in fact, has a pneumatological character: it is the life of the Church in the Holy Spirit." Again, "tradition is not merely the aggregate of dogmas, of

"inclusive Tradition" (with a capital T): "It designates," he says, "the whole of Christian faith and practice—not only doctrinal teaching but worship, norms of behaviour, living experience, sanctity—as handed down within the church from Christ and the apostles to the present day. Understood in this comprehensive way, Tradition is not to be contrasted with Holy Scripture but seen as including it; Scripture exists within Tradition."[4]

In practice, however, what the Orthodox usually call "Holy Tradition" is not a seamless robe: it has layers of authority, or a taxis of truth—a sliding scale, shall we say—beginning with what we might call the dogmatic truths of revelation attested in Scripture by the apostolic witness and distilled in the formularies of the Niceno-Constantinopolitan Creed of AD 381. Moving down the scale, we find *theologoumena*—not self-evident truths of revelation, yet matters of great theological weight and seriousness, in which appeal to Scripture is normative, though with some leeway for disagreement. Lower still down the scale, we come across what we might call "pious opinion"—speculative or popular beliefs or practices, supported by the church fathers or their successors, but not necessarily warranted in Scripture; the Feast of the Dormition of the *Theotokos*, Mary the "mother of God," would be a classic example. If we slip down even further to *adiaphora*—matters of minor significance, such as the tradition that monks should wear beards—we soon end at the bottom with mere private opinion, which has no ecclesial authority at all.[5]

These gradations, however, while perhaps offering a rubric of doctrinal distinction that merits ecumenical attention, are not germane to the retrieval of *paradosis* as the dogmatic core of the Christian faith.

D. H. Williams, like David Bebbington, the English historian, makes the case that evangelicalism is as much a child of the Enlightenment as it is a grandchild of the Reformation.[6] Consequently, there is a built-in bias toward individualism at the expense of community and tradition. This is exacerbated by evangelical missiology, which, being essentially activist, can

---

sacred institutions, and of rites which the Church preserves. It is . . . a living tradition, the unceasing revelation of the Holy Spirit in the Church" (Lossky, *The Mystical Theology of the Eastern Church* [1957], 188, 236). On Florovsky, see his *Bible, Church, Tradition* (1972).

4. Ware, "Tradition and Traditions" (1991).

5. These distinctions are not universally accepted within Orthodoxy. Some suggest slightly different scales.

6. Cf. Williams, *Retrieving the Tradition* (1999), 19; see Bebbington, *Evangelicalism in Modern Britain* (1989).

be loosed from its moorings in ecclesiology and become something outside the church that takes on a life of its own. Another feature of evangelical faith, its experientialism, though positive in itself, at times cuts adrift and sails away from doctrine, contributing to an uninformed and undernourished faith. Evangelicals, Williams claims, suffer from "theological amnesia" and this not only robs them of their past, but it also destroys their sense of identity in the here and now.[7]

And what we find when we join Williams and turn back to those nascent years, is that there is something consistent and coherent emerging that we can rightly identify as the "rule of faith." This rule, as formalized by Saint Vincent of Lérins (died c. 445), was predicated on three tests of orthodoxy: that which was accepted by (a) everyone (*universitas*), (b) always (*antiquitas*), and (c) everywhere (*consensio*), all of which were necessary for the confident affirmation of orthodoxy but none of which were sufficient tests on their own (*Commonitorium* 2). Thus, even if the faith of the church was celebrated throughout the whole world (*universitas*), if it did not go back to the apostles (*antiquitas*) it was not the faith of the church catholic. And if there was a consensus of faith (*consensio*) but it could not be traced back to apostolic origins (*antiquitas*) neither was this the true faith. But even a faith that can be traced back to early times (*antiquitas*), yet did not merit what Florovsky calls "a comprehensive consensus of the 'ancients'"[8] could not be counted as the one true faith either.

What can be said to constitute tradition, and whether Scripture and tradition can be said to cohere together as *paradosis*, will be the main focus of the rest of this chapter. Our approach will be to see what Scripture itself has to say about tradition, and then move on to how it was received and interpreted by the fathers. Following a very brief foray into post-Reformation theology, we will conclude that deep church is itself a recovering church, both in the sense that it is recovering *paradosis* and that it is recovering from its amnesia through *paradosis*.

Paradosis in Scripture and the Early Church

The language of tradition in the New Testament is encapsulated both by the noun *paradosis* itself (and its verb equivalent *paradidōmi*) and by related concepts to do with handing on and receiving (such as *paralambanō*—to

7. Williams, *Retrieving the Tradition* (1999), 9, 11.
8. Florovsky, "The Function of Tradition in the Ancient Church" (1972), 74.

take; or to receive something transmitted). The double meaning of *paradosis* as both (a) the dogmatic or apostolic *content* and (b) the dynamic *process* of passing that content on is not an interpolation of the fathers into the biblical text. It is there in the text such that we can see it for ourselves. Paul uses the word *paradosis* itself five times in his epistles. One is a negative reference to human tradition in his letter to the Colossians, where he says, "See to it that no one takes you captive . . . according to human tradition" (Col 2:8). Another is where he tells of his zeal in following the traditions of his ancestors, before he received the revelation of Jesus (Gal 1:14). And the remaining three references are all endorsements of *paradosis* (1 Cor 11:2; 2 Thess 2:15; 3:6).[9]

If we look at tradition in the first sense of embodying apostolic content, we can see it used by Paul in this way in 2 Thessalonians 2:15—"Stand firm and hold fast to the traditions [*paradosis*] that you were taught by us, either by word of mouth or by our letter."[10] (We note here, too, that this content may have been delivered orally or by letter.) Or again, in 1 Corinthians 11:2 Paul writes: "I commend you because you remember me in everything and maintain the traditions [*paradosis*] just as I handed them on [*paradidōmi*] to you." Here Paul uses both the noun and the verb form together, the content and the process of tradition— "I handed on the handed-on-things," or "I traditioned the traditions to you." In 2 Thessalonians 3:6, Paul charges: "Now we command you, brothers, in the name of our Lord Jesus Christ, to keep away from every brother who is living in idleness and not according to the tradition [*paradosis*] that they received [*paralambanō*] from us." This last reference links us to the next by its use of *paralambanō* to talk about the element of receiving that which has been handed on.

If we now turn to the second sense of *paradosis* as the process by which it is handed on, this too is used by Paul. We saw above how he does this in 1 Corinthians 11:2; again in Philippians 4:9 he writes, "Keep on doing the things that you have learned and received [*paralambanō*] and heard and seen in me, and the God of peace will be with you." But this sense of *paradosis* also appears in the Gospels. Luke writes in the introduction to

9. As an aside, it is worth mentioning that one might not notice this if one read the New International Version, for in "good" evangelical fashion it will not countenance any positive use of the word "tradition" at all.

10. The Greek word here, of course, is plural (*paradoseis*); however, for clarity and ease of reference, and to facilitate comparison, in this reference and the ones that follow the basic forms of the Greek words are used.

his gospel, "Since many have undertaken to set down an orderly account of the events that have been fulfilled among us, just as they were handed on [*paradidōmi*] to us by those who from the beginning were eyewitnesses and servants of the word" (1:1–2). Paul, again, in 1 Corinthians 15:3–4 says, "For I handed on [*paradidōmi*] to you as of first importance what I in turn had received [*paralambanō*]: that Christ died for our sins in accordance with the Scriptures, and that he was buried, and that he was raised on the third day in accordance with the scriptures." Second Timothy 2:2 has Paul using a related notion of *paradosis*: "and what you have heard from me through many witnesses entrust [*paratithēmi*] to faithful people who will be able to teach others as well."

1 Corinthians 11:23 is perhaps the most significant New Testament text on *paradosis* either as content or process, for it is linked with the centrality of the Eucharist for Christian experience. Paul says, "For I received [*paralambanō*] from the Lord what I also handed on [*paradidōmi*] to you," here again using the verb equivalent of the noun *paradosis*. Paul then begins the solemn words of commemoration of and participation in the paschal meal, "that the Lord Jesus on the night when he was betrayed took a loaf of bread, and when he had given thanks, he broke it and said, 'This is my body . . .'" (vv. 23–24).

What links these scriptural quotations is not their mode of communication, as *paradosis* is both oral and written testimony (as we saw in 2 Thess 2:15); rather, what binds them together is the authenticity of their apostolic origin. The apostolic faith itself derives its authority directly from the Lord Jesus Christ who is not only the source of the tradition but also its content (2 Cor 1:20; 4:5–6).

When we move from the New Testament record of the apostolic faith as tradition and look at the patristic understanding of *paradosis*, we note that what matters above all to the early fathers is that they are in the apostolic tradition. One of Athanasius's most successful arguments against Arius at the Council of Nicaea (AD 325), for example, was that the presbyter's doctrine refuting the eternal generation of Christ—"there was when he was not"—was an *innovation* and could not be found in the apostles or their successors in the first and second centuries.[11] If we were to apply Vincent's

---

11. See esp. Williams, *Arius* (2002), particularly the new appendix; see also standard texts such as, e.g., Kelly, *Early Christian Doctrines* (1977); Hanson, *The Search for the Christian Doctrine of God* (1988); and Chadwick, *The Church in Ancient Society* (2001).

three tests of faith—*universitas, antiquitas,* and *consensio*—to Arianism, it fails on all three counts.

However, as early as the second century a distinction began to emerge in the discourse on apostolic faith, which increasingly defined tradition as that which is oral, and Scripture as that which is written. Initially, the distinction was simply to differentiate the different modes of communication of the one true apostolic faith (*paradosis*), but in time Scripture was privileged over tradition or, as we shall argue, a better way to characterize the distinction is to say that the two modes eventually were understood to perform different but complementary functions.

The first major authority in which these distinctions are clearly operative is Irenaeus of Lyon (c. AD 130–200). A long quotation from *Adversus haereses* (*Against Heresies*) highlights his "high view" of the status of oral tradition. He says of the gnostics and their claim to a "purer truth" independent of apostolic tradition:

> But when on our side we challenge them by an appeal to that tradition which derives from the Apostles, and which is preserved in the churches by the successions of presbyters, then they oppose tradition, claiming to be wiser not only than the presbyters but even than the Apostles, and to have discovered the truth undefiled. (3.2.2)

> Those who wish to see the truth can observe in every church the tradition of the Apostles made manifest in the whole world. We can enumerate those who were appointed bishops in the churches by the Apostles, and their successors down to our own day. They never taught and never knew of such absurdities as those heretics produce . . .
> But it would be excessively tedious, in a book of this kind, to give detailed lists of the successions in all the churches. Therefore we will refute [the gnostics] . . . by pointing to the tradition of the greatest and oldest church, a church known to all men, which was founded and established at Rome by the most renowned Apostles Peter and Paul. This tradition the church has from the Apostles, and this faith has been proclaimed to all men, and has come down to our own day through the succession . . . (*Haer.* 3.3.1–2)

By contrast, a short and succinct quotation from the same document highlights the double authority of Scripture and tradition: "It comes to this, therefore, that these men do now consent neither to Scripture nor to tradition" (*Haer.* 3.2.2). For Irenaeus, then, tradition is delineated from Scripture by its mode of operation. In short, to repeat ourselves, while both modes of communication are apostolic, Scripture is *written* and tradition is *oral*.

From the second century onwards, in what, after all, was an essentially oral culture, apostolic faith was defended and supported as *both* oral tradition *and* written Scripture. Examples of this universal acceptance of the two paths of apostolic faith are numerous. In the second and third century, for example, we can move from Tertullian (c. AD 155–220) in the West who argued, "Our appeal [against heretics], therefore, must not be made to the Scriptures" (*Praescr.* 19),[12] to the mid-fourth century of Cyril of Jerusalem in the East who cautions, "But in learning the faith and in professing it, acquire and keep that only, which is now delivered to thee by the church, and which has been built up strongly out of all the Scriptures" (*Cat.* 5.12). And, around the same time, from that doughty campaigner of orthodoxy, Athanasius, we read his quotation of the words of Anthony: "Therefore, keep yourselves clean from these [the Arians] and watch over the tradition of the Fathers, and, above all, the orthodox faith in our Lord Jesus Christ, as you have learned it from the Scriptures and as you have often been put in mind of by me" (*Vit. Ant.* 89). If we move forward to the end of the fourth century, evidence from two of the Cappadocian fathers and the lesser known Epiphanius of Salamis seems to suggest on a first reading that oral tradition was considered equal in stature to written Scripture. Epiphanius tells us, for example, that "tradition must be used too, for not everything is available from the sacred Scripture. Thus the holy apostles handed some things down in Scriptures but some in traditions" (*Pan.* 61.6.5). And Gregory Nazianzus, writing concerning the innovations in doctrine of Apollinarius and his followers, insists, "Our faith has been proclaimed both in written and in unwritten form, here and in distant parts, in danger and in security. Why then do some men attempt such innovations, while others remain peaceful?" (*ep.* 101.1). And most emphatically Basil demonstrates that part of the living tradition of the apostles that had been handed on was self-evidently not to be found in Scripture:

12. Tertullian here, of course, is not arguing against the authority of Scripture, but rather that to try to dispute with the heretics—who themselves based their arguments upon the Scriptures—from those same Scriptures, was to place "both sides on a par," Scripture being the common ground. The question that he says must be asked in this case is, "With whom lies that very faith to which the Scriptures belong? From what [original Giver], and through whom, and when, and to whom, has been handed down that rule, by which men become Christians? For wherever it shall be manifest that the true Christian rule and faith shall be, *there* will likewise be the true Scriptures and expositions thereof, and [indeed] all the Christian traditions" (*ANCL*, 15:22).

> Of the beliefs and practices preserved in the church . . . we have some derived from written teaching; others we have received as delivered to us "in a mystery" [here Basil means the sacraments or the holy mysteries (*mysterion*), not secret doctrines] from the tradition of the Apostles; and both classes have the same force, for true piety. No one will dispute these; no one, at any rate, who has even the slightest experience of the institutions of the church. If we tried to depreciate the customs lacking within authority, on the ground that they have but little validity, we should find ourselves unwittingly inflicting vital injury on the gospel: or rather reducing official definition to a mere form of words (*de Sp. sanct.* 66).

But lest we be guilty of quoting too much from Eastern theologians let us end this section with a quote from the defining father of Western tradition, Augustine of Hippo (writing here c. AD 400): "As to those other things which we hold on the authority, not of Scripture, but of tradition, and which are observed throughout the whole world, it may be understood that they are held as approved and instituted either by the apostles themselves, or by plenary Councils, whose authority in the Church is most useful" (*ep.* 54.1.1).

It is time for a recapitulation in our attempt to make sense of *paradosis* as the apostolic faith handed on both in Scripture and oral tradition. The issue at stake for the fathers from the beginning of the apologetic century was never Scripture versus tradition, or writing versus orality, but the desire *to be faithful to the apostolic witness* preserved in *both* Scripture *and* tradition.

We cannot, however, ignore the probability that from the late first or early second century of the common era, and certainly from the end of the fourth century, tradition and Scripture did not—despite the rhetoric—cohere as equal authorities in the *paradosis* of the church. Scripture was without doubt by far the most senior partner in this relationship. Bishop Kallistos highlights this by concentrating on Basil.[13] For while the Cappadocian father, as we have seen, asserted the legitimacy of oral tradition alongside the text of Scripture, in fact the apostolic oral tradition that he invokes is not of the same order as the foundational truths of salvation distilled in the Niceno-Constantinopolitan Creed of AD 381, nor of the apostolic kerygma of Holy Writ. When we actually examine the list of oral traditions that Basil believes to be apostolic though not mentioned in Scripture, we find such things as the sign of the cross, blessing those to be baptized or the water in which they are baptized, turning to the east during prayer,

---

13. Ware, "Tradition and Traditions" (1991), 1013–17.

the epiclesis invoked over the holy gifts at the Eucharist, and the threefold immersion in baptism. For Basil, therefore, unwritten tradition—although apostolic in origin and thus to be embraced—is not revelatory truth but sanctioned and sanctified custom (*de Sp. sanct.* 66).

Furthermore, by the end of the fourth century it was clearly no longer possible to claim that anyone knew the apostles, as Ignatius of Antioch (died c. AD 110) probably had in the first century. Nor could anyone say, as Irenaeus was able to of his teacher, Polycarp, in the second century, that they knew someone who knew one of the twelve apostles or Paul. The demise of personal knowledge of the apostolic generation meant that oral tradition began to lose its allure and even its status as *paradosis*. It cannot be said, therefore, that the *consensus fidelium* of the church, East and West, at this time taught that oral tradition was a source of revelation (as the Council of Trent affirmed in 1546). Whereas it could be said of *paradosis* that it began as the living oral tradition of the church rather than as text (as the church chronologically preceded the Bible), it was inconceivable, once the texts of Scripture became available, that the apostolic kerygma could stand alone as tradition without biblical warrant.

We can also claim that, although the final canon of Scripture (based largely on Athanasius's list) was not ratified until the end of the fourth century, many of the written documents in circulation in the first three Christian centuries were *from their inception* treated as sacred texts as, of course, were the Jewish Scriptures (the Christian Old Testament). At the Council of Nicaea in AD 325, for example, the four Gospels were laid out in front of the Emperor Constantine and the senior bishops as the highest court of appeal for the test of orthodoxy.

The fact that the Fathers had Scripture on their minds and in their hearts is nowhere more clearly demonstrated than in the creeds and councils of the early church. They cannot be seen, therefore, as merely contingent (and hence optional) historical findings extrinsic to Scripture *for Scripture is intrinsic to them.*

By the end of the fifth century, after the ecumenical triumph of the Council of Chalcedon in 451, and following Vincent's codification of the "rule of faith," tradition was no longer identified, as it was by Irenaeus in the second century, as orality and distinguished from the Bible merely by manuscription, for it had become tied-up and tied-in with Scripture in such a way that it is more helpful to see them in symbiotic terms: Scripture in a sense is affirmed, sustained, and unfolded by tradition, but tradition is illuminated, judged, and controlled by Scripture. Together they are the content of faith: *paradosis*.

Paradosis as the dynamic process of handing on the deposit of faith was primarily seen by the Fathers of the fifth century as a function of the church. As early as the edict of toleration in 313 and the following Constantinian settlement, the church had emerged as the official guardian of the faith, which carried with it not only a positive message of "rightly discerning the truth" but also negative connotations of power-broking and authoritarian control.

Because of this negativity, D. H. Williams thinks that the Radical Reformers and their successors misread the significance of the accord between church and state.[14] Undoubtedly the church empirical stumbled and fell, but the radicals read it as a spiritual fall: a descent into apostasy. Christ, however, told the disciples that the gates of hell shall not prevail against the church (Matt 15:18), and the church elsewhere in Scripture is described by Paul as "the pillar and foundation of the truth" (1 Tim 3:15; NIV). That the church was also the vehicle for passing on that truth was taken for granted by the fathers. It simply makes no sense to view the church as a value-free or morally neutral conductor of the apostolic faith, like a conveyor belt moving the gospel on from place to place: it has to be seen as the interpretative carrier handing on—through its liturgy, piety, monastic spirituality, and its Magisterium—the faith "once for all delivered to the saints."

Georges Florovsky's view on the relationship between church as the carrier of Scripture (*paradosis* as process) and tradition (*paradosis* as content) by the time of Vincent is insightful. In his seminal article on "The Function of Tradition in the Ancient Church" he argues, on the one hand, that Vincent reflects the *consensus fidelium* of the patristic age when he declared that the apostolic faith was authorized by and contained in the "perfect" and "self sufficient" rule or canon of Scripture. On the other hand, his high view of the church—which echoes Augustine's confession, "Indeed, I should not have believed the gospel, if the authority of the Catholic Church had not moved me" (*Fund.* 5.6)—is vital to his understanding of the preservation and continuation of the rule of faith. For it was not only the Protestant Reformation that raised the question of the relationship between Scripture and private interpretations. In the early church heretics were seen as those holding private opinions inimical to the commonwealth of faith. The author of 2 Peter raises the issue where he tells the faithful, "no matter

14. See especially chap. 4 of Williams, *Retrieving the Tradition* (1999).

of prophecy in Scripture is a matter of one's own interpretation" (2 Pet 1:20). And he goes on to warn his audience that there would be false teachers among them (2 Pet 2:1). And he was right. Marcion, for example, in the second century denied the validity of the Old Testament as Scripture, and Ebionites, Sabellians, Arians, and gnostics all quoted Scripture to support their positions. Tertullian refused to debate with heretics on the ground that the Scriptures were not theirs to interpret, for the Scriptures belonged to the church that was the guardian of the deposit of faith (*Praescr.* 19).

Florovsky thinks that Vincent followed Hilary of Poitiers, the great Western theologian of the fourth century, when he said of the Scriptures that they must not only be read but must also be understood.[15] By itself tradition, for Vincent, added nothing to the revelation of God in Christ as handed down by the apostles and attested to in Scripture, but it did provide, through ecclesiastical guardianship of and faithful adherence to the apostles' teaching, the medium which alone could properly expound and interpret Scripture. According to Florovsky, tradition, for Vincent, is "Scripture rightly understood."[16]

Paradosis from the Reformation to the Present Day

If we briefly move our discussion of *paradosis* forward from the fathers to the Protestant Reformation, what we find is not a rejection of tradition per se but an attempt to curtail the power of the Magisterium as it had developed in the West, where supreme authority in the church had become invested in the pope. The Magisterial Reformers felt the way ahead was for the church as the harbinger of tradition to be subjected to the sovereignty of Scripture.

In itself, as we have seen, this was a perfectly patristic way of doing things, were it not for the humanist tendency to abrogate the authority of the church as vehicle or carrier (*paradosis* as process) of the "rule of faith" (*paradosis* as content) to the conscience of autonomous individuals. This tendency ran the risk of making every person his or her own pope (with, in fact, *far* more power to reshape Christian faith than any actual pope, constrained as popes are by the tradition), and in so doing opened the door to theological pluralism.

15. "For Scripture is not in the reading, but in the understanding," quoted in Florovsky, "Function of Tradition" (1972), 75.

16. See ibid., 73–77.

Nevertheless, while the iconoclastic energy of the Reformation arguably ran out of control, it would be quite wrong to accuse the Reformers of rejecting the tradition of the early church out of hand; for despite the rallying cry of *sola scriptura, sola fidei*, they accepted the *consensus fidelium* of the first few centuries up to and including Vincent, neither denying the efficacy nor the legitimacy of the first four great ecumenical councils nor the three historic creeds (The Nicene Creed, the Apostles Creed, and the Athanasian Creed).

They did this not because they saw these as *adiaphora*—things that did not matter one way or the other—but because they believed the christological and Trinitarian doctrines to be grounded in, consonant with, or derived from Holy Scripture. On the very same grounds, in 1869 Charles Hodge, the great Princeton systematic theologian, was able to write in his letter to Pope Pius IX turning down his invitation to be an observer at the First Vatican Council, "We regard all the doctrinal decisions of the first six ecumenical councils to be consistent with the word of God, and because of that consistency, we receive them as expressions of faith."[17]

Conclusion

Like an orphan who does not know her family history, many Christians are bereft of their past and are the poorer for it. Although Brueggemann coined the phrase "gospel amnesia" to describe the modernist turn in the church,[18] D. H. Williams has demonstrated that forgetfulness is not only a problem for liberals: it remains a difficulty for many committed Christians who have little knowledge or experience of the *paradosis* of the church. One thinks, for instance, of those evangelical who set the Bible (the divine word) and tradition (a mere human word) in conflict with each other and then claim to follow the Bible and to reject tradition. This approach is both internally incoherent (if one does not trust the tradition of the church, on what basis does one accept the canon of Scripture, given that it was the church that discerned which books should be included?) and, as we have seen, would have been utterly unintelligible to any Christians prior to the modern period. Protestants need to raise the status of tradition above the

17. Transcribed from Charles Hodge's handwritten draft. It resides in the archives of Princeton Seminary and can be accessed with the help of the Librarian for Archives and Special Collections.

18. Brueggemann, *Biblical Perspectives on Evangelism* (1993), 90–93.

level of custom and *adiaphora*. For Florovsky, ironically, the long-term consequence of the Protestant Reformation—when, as he saw it, the Bible was uncoupled from tradition—is not the demise of tradition but, alas, "the loss of the scriptural mind."[19]

Tradition cannot solely be defined, as Florovsky put it, as "Scripture rightly understood," but we think his idea flags the big question: What is the church? It is clear that we cannot have a definition of *paradosis* as handing on the tradition unless we see the church in a more positive light. And if Basil and Irenaeus were not wrong in understanding that the church hands on its treasures through its rites and practices, sacraments and pastoral care, as well as creeds, decrees of ecumenical councils, and Holy Scripture, how can we determine which rites and customs are the most appropriate for this transmission of faith? This is no small matter; for the apostolic faith to be a living one it has not only to be retrieved, it also needs to be reactivated and received. This requires a living tradition of worship, discipleship, and service. Living tradition is the provision of the spiritual environment without which the Bible cannot flourish as Scripture.

This chapter has sought to clear the ground and to lay some foundations for our exploration of deep church. We have argued that a positive appreciation of the symbiotic roles of Scripture and tradition in the life of a church that makes claims to be *apostolic* is critical. Authentic and relevant Christian faith in the present requires not simply understanding our own cultural contexts but also recovering the faith's deep roots in the past. Deep church is about remembering our future.

---

19. A paraphrase of the title of his essay, "The Lost Scriptural Mind" (1972).

4

Deep Calls to Deep

Introduction to Chapters 5–7

IN AN IMPORTANT BOOK on scriptural approaches to knowledge, *Biblical Knowing*, Dru Johnson points out that the meaning of things is not there on the surface of reality to read off, raw facts that simply are *self-evident*. To know reality we must *interpret* it and for that we need guides, those who already possess some relevant knowledge. Parents, teachers, and other experts help us to make sense of the world, leading us on a journey toward greater understanding. This resonates with the traditional Christian approach to the role of Scripture and tradition explained in the last chapter.

Johnson argues that Scripture presents a surprisingly consistent general approach toward knowledge. The biblical pattern, he maintains, fundamentally involves guides/instructors/prophets that have *authoritative understanding* of the matters in question and who are *authorized* to speak to the matters concerned by the relevant authorities. Such guides can lead others in a process of learning toward knowledge. People who are in a fiducially bound relationship with these guides can come to a correct understanding by *listening attentively* to the guides and *putting into practice* what they say. One can err—and thus fail to progress toward knowledge—by either listening to the wrong authority (i.e., one who does not actually understand the matters at hand) or by failing to follow the guide's teaching.

Knowledge in the Bible is not simply a matter of affirming the right set of propositions about a matter: "knowing *that such and such is the case.*" Knowledge is fundamentally connected with a process of listening to a guide and practicing what they say; it is fundamentally about a certain kind of committed posture of the self. This is as true in matters of religious devotion as it is in matters of practical skills (such as woodwork or baking) and theoretical understanding (such as mathematics).

In Eden God himself served as the guide for Adam and Eve and it was in listening to the wrong authority (the serpent) and in failing to follow the instructions of the right authority (God) that Adam and Eve fell away from the knowledge of God. From Exodus to Deuteronomy Moses served as the authoritative and authorized guide for Israel. Israel could know the LORD if they *listened* to Moses' God-given teaching and *put it into practice*. Johnson shows that this dual theme of "listening to the voice" and "obeying" as the means to know the LORD are driven home time and time and time again. Subsequently the written Law of Moses served alongside prophetic interpreters (climaxing in Jesus, the prophet like Moses anticipated in Deuteronomy).

What this pattern underscores is that knowing God is not simply a matter of believing true information about God. Such a view is hopelessly reductionist. As James says, even the demons can do that (Jas 2:18). Knowing God is a journey that involves walking in the ways of the LORD. As Jesus said, "If you hold to my teaching, you are really my disciples. *Then you will know the truth* and the truth will set you free" (John 8:31–32). Knowing the truth follows on from walking as a disciple of Jesus. The person with wisdom, said the Lord, is the one who "*hears* these words of mine and *does* them" (Matt 7:24). Failure to obey is failure to know aright.

This approach to knowing God is not dissimilar to that of Søren Kierkegaard. He was strongly allergic to the antiseptic Enlightenment attempts to use so-called "objective reason" to prove the truths of Christianity. Christian truth is essentially concerned with the *impact* and *relevance* of truth for our existence and life—truth is *transformative*. It cannot be appropriated through the dispassionate mode of objectivity: "from the [rational] demonstration nothing follows for me."[1] For Kierkegaard Christian "truth is subjectivity."[2] By this he does not mean that Christian truth makes no objective claims—about God or Jesus—but rather that such truth is only fulfilled, is only itself, when it engages me existentially and becomes "true for me." Kyle Roberts writes,

> For Kierkegaard, the truth of Christianity cannot be abstracted from existence—and therefore from people who appropriate and

1. Kierkegaard, *Christian Discourses* (1997), 191.

2. A claim explored in Kierkegaard, *Concluding Unscientific Postscript* (1992).

embody it (followers of Christ). Therefore, the main question is not about the doctrine or the truth of the doctrine as such, but rather about the way in which one relates personally to the doctrine: whether in belief, trust, and obedience, or skepticism, doubt, or mere intellectual curiosity. As he states, "truth has always had many loud proclaimers, but the question is whether a person will in the deepest sense acknowledge the truth, will allow it to permeate his whole being."[3]

Christians are not simply those that make certain propositional claims about God and Jesus. Anyone who claims that such an objective "faith" amounts to Christian faith is fundamentally mistaken. Christian faith is "belief *in* . . ." and not merely "belief *that* . . ."; it is a trust and commitment to love God and to love others. In other words, knowing the truth of Christianity is no mere conceptual knowledge but is a knowledge embodied in a way of life—a life of worship and holy living.

The journey toward knowing is also a risk. There is always the danger that one may be listening to the wrong guide. There is no failsafe way to avoid that risk. One must simply begin a journey in trust. Roberts, again on Kierkegaard:

> [K]nowledge is never complete because existence is never complete. . . . [O]bjectively speaking, despite the passion of one's religious convictions, one could always be "mistaken." Christ was a historical being. But history lies outside of the realm of the provable. The Bible mediates, in part, our objective (and narrative) knowledge of God and Christ. But the Bible cannot be proven to be absolutely historically factual, objectively speaking. There can be no objective "proof" for the viability of Christianity—objective certainty about the religious is elusive. Human beings cannot step outside of their limits (geography, history, language, etc.) and attain a universal perspective on reality. When *God* is the issue of knowledge, one's relation to the subject matter is best (and religiously speaking, *only*) approached through the passionate subjectivity of faith—not through objective reflection. . . . Christianity is an "existence-communication"; it cannot be truly understood apart from existing in it and without being deeply, personally transformed by it.[4]

---

3. Roberts, *Emerging Prophet* (2013), 39. Quoting Kierkegaard, *The Concept of Anxiety* (1981), 138.

4. Roberts, *Emerging Prophet* (2013), 41.

We need to appreciate that right belief, understood as an existential commitment to the Triune God, is not simply something that is present or absent. It is a lifelong journey. Dru Johnson again on Scripture's model of knowing God: "Knowing is a diachronic process, not a punctiliar moment in the narrative's logic, although it often comes to heightened points of illumination (e.g., Gen 2:23; Exod 14:31; Deut 4:35; Mark 8:29–33)."[5] Consider the relationship of knowing another person. There is a sense in which you can say of a friend, "I know John," but there is another sense in which your knowing John is an ongoing journey of *coming to know* John in deeper and deeper ways. In *that* sense your knowledge of John is not simply present or absent but is a complex, deepening knowledge. It is the same with the relationship of trusting another person. You can say, "I trust John," but in another sense trust is something that grows and deepens with time and experience. Right belief in the Father, Son, and Spirit is the same way. Belief in God is like a dimmer switch on a light. There is indeed an on and an off mode but the on mode comes in a wide range of degrees of brightness. As the man with the epileptic son said to Jesus, "Lord, I believe. Help my unbelief" (Mark 9:24). Right belief is the *on* mode—the positive orientation of the heart toward trust in the Triune God. However, it is a journey of growing brightness. This is why Søren Kierkegaard would not have said that he was a Christian. He would have said that he was *becoming* a Christian. And there is one sense in which that is quite correct.

Faith, as Augustine observed, is a prerequisite for understanding. Anselm (c. 1033–1109) expressed this insight as follows: "I do not try, Lord, to attain Your lofty heights, because my understanding is in no way equal to it. But I do desire to understand your truth a little, that truth that my heart believes and loves. For I do not seek to understand so that I may believe; but I believe so that I may understand."[6] And as the understanding of what we believe grows so our belief itself matures. One could sum up Augustine's and Anselm's approach to faith as follows: "Lord, I believe that you are, but I am not really sure what that means. Please enlighten me some more so that I may better know and love you." The Trinity is an obvious case in point. The Creed affirms it and Christians believe it but there has never been a Christian that has really understood the Trinity. We believe in the God who is triune but what exactly is it for God to be triune? That we do not know.

---

5. Johnson, *Biblical Knowing* (2013), 200.

6. Anselm, *Proslogion* 1 (in Anselm, *Major Works* [1998], 87).

Furthermore, it is not an accident that the Creed begins, "we believe *in* one God . . ." and not "we believe *that there is* one God . . ." The Creed is a communal expression of faith in the God of the gospel. So while the church believes the Creed, it does not believe *in* the Creed; it believes *in* the Triune God. Of course, to consciously believe *in* this God requires one to believe *that* this God is, but the primary focus for Christianity is the active commitment of trust in this God. The propositional "belief" is ordered toward and derives its significance from this existentially engaged faith. We will explore this more in the next chapter.

The Indivisibility of Right Belief, Right Worship, and Right Action

The church has historically appreciated the indivisibility of right belief, right worship, and right living. All three are of the essence of *faith in* Jesus, of *knowing* God. They can be conceptually distinguished but such an intellectual act of abstraction is artificial, dislocating faith from its setting in life, and is in danger of obscuring as much as it reveals.

Right belief, as explained above, is inconceivable apart from right worship and right action. Right belief is a posture of the self that, when directed Godward, manifests *as* prayer and praise. Worship is, as it were, right-belief-engaging-God. There is a deep Christian instinct that if someone claims to believe in the God of Jesus Christ and yet does not worship and praise and pray to that God then that person's claim to believe is fraudulent. At best they have a mere propositional faith; although, even then, how any human being could truly believe *that* "God was in Christ reconciling the world to himself" and yet refuse to make any personal response to such belief makes no sense at all to the Christian heart.

Orthodoxy is also joined at the hip to *orthopraxy*. Saint Paul speaks of "faith *expressing itself* through love" (Gal 5:6). That is to say, works of love *are* faith in action, or right-belief-engaging-other-people. And apart from such right action one cannot speak of *right* faith. Consider the story of the friends who brought the paralytic man to Jesus and lowered him through the roof. Matthew tells us that "when Jesus *saw their faith*, he said . . ." (Matt 9:2). By seeing their faith Jesus was not seeing their inner mental states—their assent to certain facts about himself; he was seeing their faith *manifest in their actions*. The inseparability of right faith and right action is underscored again and again in the Bible and in the tradition. Here, for instance, is Calvin on the importance of practice to faith in Exodus 4: "But we shall presently see how fickle and infirm was their belief [Exod 4:31]. It is plain, from its levity and inconstancy, that it was without any living root. But it is not unusual that the word belief should be improperly applied to a mere assent and disposition to believe, which speedily passes away."[7] All this is to say that right belief is not *right* belief if it is not manifest in right worship and right action.

In the same way, right worship cannot be *right* worship if it is not a manifestation of right belief and accompanied by right practice. Consider: in ancient Israel there was the constant threat of the covenant people worshiping other gods. The Bible is clear that such worship is wrong for Israel because it is not directed to the God of Israel; it grew out of misdirected faith. But the Bible *also* condemns worship of *Yhwh*, the true God, that is not based on right belief. Consider the episode of the golden calf (Exod 32–34). That statue was intended to be an image of Yhwh (Exod 32:5), not a foreign god. Yet it was rejected because Yhwh should and could not be represented in such images (Deut 5:8).

On the other hand, even when Israel's worship was directed to the right God—*Yhwh*—and was performed following all the authorized rituals, if it was not accompanied by obedience to God's torah, by embodied acts of love and justice, then it was roundly rejected (see chapter 6). At a superficial level such Israelites were orthodox but at a deeper level their deeds demonstrated otherwise.

Spiraling Upwards

Christian faith—that orientation of the heart that manifests itself in right belief, right worship, and right action—is a dynamic and developing thing in which these three dimensions impact each other. What we believe will influence our worship and actions; our worship, in turn, will reshape our beliefs and actions; our actions will feedback into our worship and faith. Ideally, there should be a virtuous spiral in which we grow toward the knowledge of God in Christ as our belief, worship, and living inter-act and we are conformed closer and closer to the image of Christ. Life, of course, is rarely so neat and the road has many twists and turns, ups and downs.

The chapters that follow explore this threefold cord of traditional Christian faith. But the vital point we have sought to underline here by

7. Calvin, *Four Last Books of Moses* (1950), 68.

way of introduction is that while we can extract each strand in that cord in order to better examine it, the cord only exists when the strands are combined and intertwined. With that warning in mind, let us take some time to examine right belief, right worship, and right action.

5

Deep Faith

Orthodoxia *as Right Believing*

THE COMMUNITY OF CHRIST-FOLLOWERS has always been a very diverse faith community. From the very first those who confessed Jesus as Messiah and Lord worked out this confession in diverse local contexts with diverse theological emphases and variations in practice. But in the midst of legitimate diversity there was also unity—a common story of Jesus' life, death, resurrection, and ascension; a common initiation rite (baptism) into a common commitment to a common Lord; common worship practices (centered around the God of Israel and Jesus his Messiah, celebrated in a common meal of bread and wine); and many shared values deriving from this Jesus-shaped story.

At the very heart of the earliest Jesus-community was what they called the *evangelion* (the gospel). This gospel was a story about what the God of Israel had done for Israel and for the world in Jesus, the Son of God. Across the different traditions of early Christ-belief represented in the New Testament we find a common story of Jesus—in whom Yhwh was uniquely manifest—crucified, buried, raised from the dead, and ascended into heaven. That was the very heart of the Jesus movement and it has remained such to this very day.

Now it is certainly true that Christians have often been tempted to shift their focus from existential faith *in* Christ to essentialist faith statements *about* him, and to the extent that we have done so we have arguably betrayed the gospel, for churches have become married to their truth claims as if they, rather than the person of Christ, were the *sine qua non* of faith.

These claims over the centuries have hardened into rubicons, which today Christians in the fragmented denominations of Christendom find it hard to cross, embedded as they are in their ecclesiastical enclosures and theological fiduciary frameworks. The heart of the faith is a living relationship with a living God, revealed in Christ. Faith in Jesus is, first and foremost, an existential commitment to and trust in Jesus; "belief *in* . . ." and not simply "belief *that* . . ." As Erasmus put it, "You will not be damned for not knowing whether the Spirit proceeds from one origin only, or from both the Father and the Son."[1]

Nevertheless, from the very beginning Jesus-believers appreciated that to have existential faith *in* Jesus one must believe certain things *about* Jesus. For instance, you cannot trust Jesus to redeem you if you do not believe that Jesus is, as a matter of fact, in a position to do so. And believing that Jesus is in a position to redeem you presumes your commitment to a whole set of beliefs about *who Jesus is* and *what he did* that put him in the position to redeem you. In other words, "belief in . . ." presupposes "belief that . . ." So although living Christian faith is certainly not subscription to a set of propositions about God and Jesus, it nevertheless does presuppose a gospel narrative that does include propositional truth claims. From the very earliest days certain truth claims have been understood to be critically important—and their denial was seen as a threat to the very gospel itself. Notice, for instance, how John says that those who deny that Christ came "in the flesh" are anti-Christs (1 John 4:1–3). Why? Because the *real humanity* of Jesus is of critical importance if he is to redeem humanity. As Gregory of Nazianzus put it in the fourth century, "that which he has not assumed he has not healed" (*ep.* 101.5).

Now one of the consequences of the modernist relegation of "religion" to the private sphere is that theological claims are simply seen as personal opinions that cannot aspire to public truth. They are either simply false (as "real" truth, i.e., scientifically-testable truth) or, if they have truth-value, it is either person-relative or unknowable. As such, the virtue of "tolerance" is often held forth as the dominant virtue that Christians ought to display on issues of theological disagreement. We should be indifferent (or even happy) that others have very different views about God and Jesus and we should not get uppity about it. Of course, it is easy to call for tolerance of all theological opinions if one is indifferent about such claims. But if one

---

1. Erasmus, Preface to the *Works of Hilary* (1642). This, of course, is not to say that the issue Erasmus mentions is not important (see Appendix 1).

really believes (a) that certain statements about God and Jesus are *true* and (b) that their truth *matters* then such indifference is not a live option and some modes of tolerance may be considered vice rather than virtue. For instance, although St Paul strongly pushed the virtue of tolerance between believers on matters adiaphora (Rom 14) when he thought the very salvation of people was put under threat by theological claims that undermined the gospel his attitude was not so live-and-let-live (Gal 1:8)!

The question is, which are the matters that Jesus-believers can agree to disagree on and which are the issues upon which the faith itself stands or falls? Here, for Christians, the gospel—the story of God's salvation of the world through the incarnation, life, death, resurrection, and ascension of Jesus—is the heart of the matter. The closer a theological claim is to that core story the more significant it is. And it was precisely this criteria that lay at the heart of attempts in the early church to define which views were orthodox and which heretical. The concern was always to reject beliefs that were seen to undermine, even if not intentionally, the gospel itself. And that gospel was the message that had been passed on in the living tradition since the days of the apostles. So the common tradition was central in identifying the contours of the narrative.

As mentioned in chapter 2, Saint Vincent of Lérins set forth his "general and guiding principle for distinguishing the true Catholic Faith from the degraded falsehoods of heresy." The problem as he saw it was that, as diverse heretics have shown, Holy Scripture is open to all sorts of different interpretations. How then can we discern truth in such matters? What is needed, says Vincent, is a guide for the orthodox interpretation of the Bible and that guide is the interpretations of the church universal—i.e., "that which has been believed everywhere, always, and by all (*quod ubique, quod semper, quod ab omnibus*). . . . We shall follow universality if we acknowledge that one Faith to be true which the whole church throughout the world confesses; antiquity if we in no wise depart from those interpretations which it is clear that our ancestors and fathers proclaimed; consent, if in antiquity itself we keep following the definitions and opinions of all, or certainly nearly all, bishops and doctors alike" (*Comm.* 4.1–3).

The Nicene Creed has served as the formal distillation of the heart of the faith catholic since the fourth and fifth centuries.[2] (See Appendix 1 for

2. While we acknowledge that there are other very important creeds in the church—most especially the Apostles' Creed and the Athanasian Creed—the Nicene Creed is the only *ecumenically agreed upon* creed, accepted by *both* Western *and* Eastern churches. (The Apostles Creed and the Athanasian Creed are recognized in the West but not in the

the text of the Creed.) But this development was not an alien imposition onto the faith but the natural climax of a process of development internal to the nature of Christianity. The ecumenical Creed (or, as the Orthodox refer to it, *Symbolon*[3]) in its original (325 AD) and modified (381 AD) forms was preceded by and based upon earlier, more local creeds in both the Greek East and the Latin West and those in turn were preceded by ancient Christian practices associated with catechesis and baptism.

Baptism and the Heart of the Faith

The source of the river that became the Nicene Creed is the New Testament articulations of who Jesus was and what he was about. Already in the earliest layers of the tradition we can find teaching about Jesus that has all the signs of formal shaping for oral transmission (1 Cor 15:3–7; Rom 1:3–4; 1 Tim 3:16). We find similar creed-like summaries of faith in the early second-century letters of Ignatius of Antioch (Ign. *Eph.* 18.2; Ign. *Trall.* 9; Ign. *Smyrn.* 1.1–2). Yet these earliest summaries of the faith are Jesus-focused. The Trinitarian shape came a little later.

During the third and fourth centuries, before the standardizing of the ecumenical Creed, candidates for baptism were instructed on the beliefs of the church by local bishops expounding local creeds: "Creeds did not originate, then, as 'tests of orthodoxy,' but as summaries that were traditional to each local church and which in detail varied from place to place."[4] Yet, despite the variety, there was a clear common core—a three-part structure based around the persons of Father, Son, and Spirit as they are revealed in the biblical narrative of the good news. Indeed, the shape of both the early and later creeds reflects the shape of the ritual of baptism itself. On the basis of Matthew 28:19 (baptizing disciples "in the name of the Father, the Son, and the Holy Spirit") the practice developed of putting three questions to the candidate:

East.) As such it is the most important Christian creed.

3. A *symbolon* was one half of a broken object that could serve to verify the authenticity of its other half when the two were put together. In the same way the creed served as a *symbolon* to check the genuine Christian compatibility of the beliefs of those who professed to be followers of the Christ. The word *creed*, on the other hand, comes from the Latin *credo*, "I believe."

4. Young, *The Making of the Creeds* (1991), 3.

Do you believe in God the Father Almighty?

Do you believe in Christ Jesus, the Son of God, who was born of the Holy Spirit of the Virgin Mary, and was crucified under Pontius Pilate, and was dead and buried, and rose again the third day, alive from the dead, and will come to judge the living and the dead?

Do you believe in the Holy Spirit, and the holy church, and the resurrection of the flesh? (Hippolytus, *Apostolic Tradition* 21)[5]

The candidate replied in the affirmative and was dipped in the water after each question—one plunge for each person, Father, Son, and Spirit. (This practice was universal in the East, and remains so today.) This baptismal practice and the catechesis associated with it is clearly that from which later, more elaborate creeds, developed. In other words, the Nicene Creed had its roots in discipleship and worship.

The Rule of Faith

Prebaptismal instruction may also underlie the rule (*kanon*) of faith, a narrative summary of the core of the Christian belief, which is expressed differently by different early Christian teachers, but beneath all the diversity is a clear common basic narrative. We shall consider three articulations of it from the second and third centuries.

Writing from Gaul, Irenaeus (died c. 202) in *The Demonstration of the Apostolic Preaching* calls on his audience to "keep the rule of faith unswervingly, and perform the commandments of God" (*Dem.* 3). This faith calls us to remember first of all that we have been baptized "in the name of God the Father, and in the name of Jesus Christ, the Son of God, [who was] incarnate, and died, and was raised, and in the Holy Spirit of God" (*Dem.* 3). Notice again the Trinitarian gospel-shape to baptism. He goes on to explain the three articles of the rule of faith:

And this is the order of our faith, the foundation of [the] edifice and the support of [our] conduct:

God, the Father, uncreated, uncontainable, invisible, one God, the Creator of all: this is the first article of our faith.

5. The Hippolytan authorship of this text is contested among liturgical scholars.

And the second article: the Word of God, the Son of God, Christ Jesus our Lord, who was revealed by the prophets according to the character of their prophecy and according to the economies of the Father, by whom all things were made, and who, in the last times, to recapitulate all things, became a man amongst men, visible and palpable, in order to abolish death, to demonstrate life and to effect communion between God and man.

And the third article: the Holy Spirit, through whom the prophets prophesied and the patriarchs learnt the things of God and the righteous were led in the path of righteousness, and who, in the last times, was poured out in a new fashion upon the human race renewing man, throughout the world, to God. (*Dem.* 6)

This story is not simply of intellectual interest. The very experience of salvation, through baptism, "takes place through these three articles, granting us regeneration unto God the Father through His Son by the Holy Spirit . . . Thus, without the Spirit it is not [possible] to see the Word of God, and without the Son one is not able to approach the Father" (*Dem.* 7). Irenaeus elsewhere spoke of the Son and the Spirit as the two hands of the Father. By means of this analogy he sought to communicate that *all* of the Father's interaction with creation is mediated through his Son and his Spirit. The Father comes to creation through his Son and in his Spirit; creation, in turn, comes to the Father through the Son and in the Spirit.

On what basis can Irenaeus claim that this "rule" captures the essentials of Christ-faith? Because, as we saw in chapter 2, this rule of faith was, he said, passed on from the apostles to the elders, their successors, and from them to Irenaeus's generation. So there is a *direct* line Irenaeus can trace from the teachings of the apostles to the teachings in the churches of his own day. This teaching, unlike the secret teachings of the gnostics, is public and it has been consistently taught in the churches founded by the apostles.

As Tertullian (c. 160–c. 225), based in North Africa, noted, "This rule, as it will be proved, was taught by Christ, and raises amongst ourselves no other questions than those which heresies introduce, and which make men heretics." He continues:

Now, with regard to this rule of faith—that we may from this point acknowledge what it is which we defend—it is, you must know, that which prescribes the belief that there is one only God, and that He is none other than the Creator of the world, who produced all things out of nothing through His own Word, first of all sent forth; that this Word is called His Son, *and*, under the name of God, was seen "in diverse manners" by the patriarchs, heard at all times in the prophets, at last brought down by the Spirit and Power of the Father into the Virgin Mary, was made flesh in her womb, and, being born of her, went forth as Jesus Christ; thenceforth He preached the new law and the new promise of the kingdom of heaven, worked miracles; having been crucified, He rose again the third day; (then) having ascended into the heavens, He sat at the right hand of the Father; sent instead of Himself the Power of the Holy Ghost to lead such as believe; will come with glory to take the saints to the enjoyment of everlasting life and of the heavenly promises, and to condemn the wicked to everlasting fire, after the resurrection of both these classes shall have happened, together with the restoration of their flesh. This rule, as it will be proved, was taught by Christ, and raises amongst ourselves no other questions than those which heresies introduce, and which make men heretics. (Tertullian, *Praescr.* 13)

Notice that he is not passing any new information on to his readers; he presupposes that his audience *already knows* the teachings he speaks of (note, "you must know"). This reinforces our impression that this was *basic* teaching communicated prior to baptism.

Moving onto third-century Egypt, Origen (184/85–253/54) set great store in the rule of faith as the guide for all Christian theologians. Origen's version shares an unmistakable common shape with those of Tertullian's and Irenaeus. He outlines it in the Preface to *On First Principles*:

The particular points clearly delivered in the teaching of the apostles are as follow:—

First, that there is one God, who created and arranged all things, and who, when nothing existed, called all things into being—God from the first creation and foundation of the world . . . This just and good God, the Father of our Lord Jesus Christ, Himself gave the law and the prophets, and the Gospels, being also the God of the apostles and of the Old and New Testaments.

Secondly, that Jesus Christ Himself, who came (into the world), was born of the Father before all creatures; that, after He had been the servant of the Father in the creation of all things—For by Him were all things made—He in the last times, divesting Himself (of His glory), became a man, and was incarnate although God, and while made a man remained the God which He was; that He

> assumed a body like to our own, differing in this respect only, that it was born of a virgin and of the Holy Spirit: that this Jesus Christ was truly born, and did truly suffer, and did not endure this death common (to man) in appearance only, but did truly die; that He did truly rise from the dead; and that after His resurrection He conversed with His disciples, and was taken up (into heaven).

> Then, *thirdly*, the apostles related that the Holy Spirit was associated in honour and dignity with the Father and the Son. . . . (Origen, *Princ.* 1.4)

He then proceeds to outline other parts of the teachings of the church on the soul, eternal life and eternal punishment, freewill, sin, the devil and his angels, the temporal beginning and end of creation (*Princ.* 1.5–7). The point of Origen's outlining of the apostolic core of the faith is simply to draw a clear line between those central issues on which Christians are agreed and matters on which there is legitimate disagreement and diverse speculations (*Princ.* 1.2).

What is impossible to miss is that the early churches from Gaul to Egypt shared a common core of beliefs that represented the very heart of Christian belief. Variety in expression of that core was permitted—we even find diverse presentations of the rule within works by a single author, such as Irenaeus—but the basic elements were fixed. That same core was manifest in the initiation rite of baptism and found its natural development in the later Nicene Creed.

The belief-core is not simply a set of theological propositions; a list of things to believe. It is, first and foremost, a *story* presented in succinct and easy to remember summary form. This story in all its diverse expressions has a common Trinitarian shape, even though it does not explore the intricacies of Trinitarian theology. It also has a common focus on the story of Jesus, anticipated by Israel's law and prophets, and now witnessed to by his apostles.

From the Rule of Faith to the Creeds

As we have seen Christian baptism had a biblically-rooted triune shape from the first century onwards (Matt 28:18; *Did.* 7). That practice, instituted by Jesus, in turn shaped the articulation of the faith of the church. The rule of faith and subsequently the earliest creeds in all their diversity reflected this common heart.

While the articulations of the rule of faith and the earliest creeds were developed to summarize the content of Christian faith with the purpose of communicating it to new converts, it was no surprise that when alternative versions of Christianity appeared on the scene the doctrinal summaries were used to sort the wheat from the chaff; to discern authentic Christian beliefs from versions that deviated from the core. And as various new and challenging teachings appeared the churches were forced to confront all sorts of questions about their faith that had not previously needed clarification. The process of discussion and clarification was often heated but through it the faith was shaped in a more precise form.[6] The later Nicene Creed aimed to agree on a standard shape of the faith across all the churches with apostolic foundations. The challenges posed as Christians reflected further on the narrative led to some fundamental disagreements and further attempts to clarify what was and what was not meant.

The Nicene Creed has become the core statement of orthodox Christian faith affirmed by Orthodox, Catholic, and mainstream Protestant churches to this day. It was the line in the sand that the churches drew in their attempt to defend the gospel story. Our contention is that it remains such today. We are not suggesting that the church does not need to say more and to continue exploring the faith as new challenges and questions arise. Our point is simply that all such ongoing explorations take place within the constraints of this ecumenical landmark in the tradition.

In Defense of the Creed

Creeds often take a fair amount of flack. In the minds of many people they are lifeless sets of "things to believe" that substitute for authentic heart-felt faith; they epitomize outward "religion" obsessed with form and ritual, as opposed to inward devotion. For some they are seen to foster a propositional approach to faith that focuses on the primacy of assent to certain claimed facts. Others see them as a source of oppression, the top-down imposition by powerful ecclesiastical hierarchies of what Christians are

6. Luke Bretherton helpfully imagines Christian doctrine and practice like an immune system that grows over time and develops through both internal and external challenges: "An immune system sometimes rejects and sometimes incorporates elements of those viruses and diseases it confronts," just as Christianity in the pursuit of health and balance, reconfigures as it confronts its challenges. It seeks to rearrange itself to maintain equilibrium, and to grow, change shape, and adapt without breaking apart. This is essential for a healthy body" (Bretherton, "Beyond the Emerging Church" [2007], 50–51).

compelled to affirm. Framed in those terms creeds do not resonate with the modern world, with its focus on the individual's authority to determine what she or he chooses to believe.

We wish to present creeds differently. The great ecumenical Creed is, we suggest, an instrument of the Holy Spirit to help keep the church focused on key aspects of the gospel message. A few points of orientation are in order.

1. The Creed is indeed concerned with certain critical assertions about God and salvation history—assertions that Christians have historically maintained as central—but it is oriented toward the primacy of *existentially committed* belief: "We believe *in* one God . . ." It is in no way a charter for a dead, intellectualized faith. Remember that in the life of the church historically and still today the Creed is embedded within the wider context of acts of *spiritual devotion* and *worship*.

2. The Creed does not point toward itself but beyond itself, like a sign. It is not valued for its own sake but for the sake of that to which it testifies.

3. The Creed does indeed contain propositions—that Jesus was crucified under Pontius Pilate, that he was buried, and so on—but they are misunderstood if they are thought to be simple lists of items to believe. On the contrary, they are in fact *narrative summaries* pointing to the grand story of the triune God's activity in creation; in the ministry, death, resurrection, and ascension of Christ; in the church; and in the future with the return of Christ and the new creation. The Creed is, of course, not narrative in form nor does it intend to substitute for the biblical narrative to which it points. Rather it serves as an interpretative summary of the core aspects of the story. The Creed, in other words, is not offered as a simple list of doctrinal beliefs for Christians to tick off and feel smug about. It is a testimony to the primacy of the biblical narrative, pointing Christians back to the Bible and offering markers for its Christian interpretation. The Creed was never a substitute for Scripture nor intended to add anything to Scripture. Rather, it was created to encapsulate the core of the apostolic understanding of Scripture's central message.

4. The Creed is not an attempt to reduce God to a set of sentences, nor an attempt to explain God. The Fathers were well aware that the God to whom the Creed bears testimony is the transcendent Creator "who dwells in unapproachable light, whom no one has seen or can see" (1 Tim 6:16).

But the Creed does not dispel mystery; if anything, it preserves it. Take the incarnation—the claim that the divine Logos "became flesh." That is a *mind-bending* claim, pushing reason over the edge. There are various ways to soften the rational offence—to claim that Jesus was not really human (Docetism) or not fully human (Apollinarianism); to claim that Jesus was not divine (Ebionism, Adoptionism, Arianism); to claim that Jesus was actually two persons, the human Jesus and the divine Word, in one body (Nestorianism).[7] All these suggestions were sensible proposals offered in sincerity. However, the church rejected all of them because, although they may remove the logical problems, they also (unintentionally) undermine critical aspects of the biblical witness and the theo-logic of the gospel itself. It is *essential* that Jesus is *fully divine* and *fully human*; that he is *one person*—not two—but that his (fully) human nature and his (fully) divine nature are not confused and blended into some hybrid. But how is that possible? It is so *crazy!* We don't know and the Creed never tries to explain it. Our point here is simply that it is precisely a *refusal* to remove mystery at the expense of central gospel affirmations that motivates the Creed.

5. The Creed does define boundaries for orthodox Christian faith, but those boundaries are surprisingly wide. They are not attempts to micromanage what Christians must think but are more akin to the fence along a national border. Within the boundaries of a country there are a lot of places one can go. The fences say, "whatever you do in here you are doing within this country but if you cross that border then you have crossed outside the bounds of the country." For instance, it is core for Christian faith that Jesus died for our sins. To deny that is to move outside the boundaries of authentic Christian beliefs. However, there are multiple different ways of trying to understand the claim that Jesus died for our sins and all of that diversity is permitted within the bounds of orthodoxy. The same goes for all sorts of different areas of theology.

6. Orthodoxy may be a large tent but it is not infinitely large. Boundaries do need to be drawn and this, we maintain, is a *good* thing. If Christianity can be anything at all then it is nothing at all. The Creed protects the shape of the faith across time and space, maintaining its continuity with the apostolic message. It does not freeze the message in time because it must be understood afresh in each generation and each fresh context. The Creed

---

7. The controversies surrounding Nicea and its creed rumbled on in the church until the fourth ecumenical council, the Council of Chalcedon in 451.

contains a surplus of meaning that can speak a good word to the church in any time or place. But it cannot mean just anything and everything. All fresh interpretations have to be firmly grounded in the tradition of interpretations in the church so far. If they break free from that then they lose the claim to be authentic Christian interpretations.

7. The ecumenical Creed serves a unifying purpose because all the main groupings within the Christian church—Orthodox, Catholic, and Protestant—affirm it. This is not insignificant. Christians disagree about an awful lot of things—praying to saints, who may be baptized, who may administer the Eucharist, the details of Christ's return, and so on—but the centrality of the Creed means that in spite of all this disagreement there is unity on the central issues. Those Protestants that have tried to sideline the Creed have actually harmed ecumenical relations in so doing. The Orthodox, for instance, are quite clear that there can be no Christian unity at the cost of central gospel truths.

8. Many point out that the Creed has "holes" in it that a robust Christian theology needs to fill. For instance, it leaps from creation to the virgin birth, making no mention of God's way with Israel. Similarly, it leaps from Jesus' birth to his death and makes no mention of his kingdom ministry, which occupies most of the space in the Gospels. There are three things we would say in reply. First, of course the Creed could say more. It is not seeking to say *everything* that Christians have to say; it is, rather, laying out the fundamental contours of the Christian belief in the triune God revealed in Jesus. It is not the final word about Christian beliefs and practices but it is an essential dogmatic statement about the Godness of the Spirit and the Son with the Father and of the humanity of Jesus. Second, what the Creed does say is intended to provide the normative theological framework within which everything else should be understood. As such it provides us with the context within which we understand the story of Israel or the ministry of Jesus or the doctrine of sin or the theology of humanity or whatever else we care to consider. Finally, the Creed is the tip of a theological iceberg with implicit links to all sorts of theological themes not overtly discussed. Take the missing story of Israel. The Creed does allude to it. Consider first an oblique reference to the central prayer of Israel, the *shema*, in the following words: "We believe in one God . . . maker of heaven and earth. . . . We believe in one Lord Jesus Christ, through whom all things were made." Behind this part of the Creed lie Paul's words in 1 Cor 8:6, "for us there is one God . . .

from whom all things come . . . and one Lord, Jesus Christ through whom all things exist." And 1 Cor 8:6, as numerous NT scholars have pointed out, is an interpretation of the *shema*: "Hear, O Israel: The Lord our God, Yhwh is one" (Deut 6:4). For Paul, Jesus is included within the identity of the one God of Israel, hence his radical take on the *shema*. The Creed preserves this Pauline interpretation of Israel's prayer thereby implying the bigger story of Israel. That bigger story can also be seen in the words "Lord Jesus *Christ*," for the title Christ (Heb. Messiah) refers to the promised ruler of Israel and the world spoken of by Israel's prophets.[8] To unpack this title requires that bigger story. Again, little phrases such as "he rose again, *according to the Scriptures*" refer to the holy texts of ancient Israel (what Christians call the Old Testament) and thereby gesture at the story of Israel contained in those texts and also at the christological interpretation of them taught to the church by Jesus (Luke 24:25–27). Our point is that the Creed does not explicitly tell the story of Israel but it does gesture to it and require its telling. Thus the church does indeed need to give a good account of God's way with Israel and we should not mistake the lack of that account in the Creed as indicating otherwise.

9. To say that those who transgress aspects of the Creed have moved beyond the bounds of authentic Christian beliefs is not to say that such people will not be saved nor even that they are not real Christians. There is an important distinction to be made between holding heretical opinions—opinions that the church has excluded as being outside the bounds of orthodoxy—and being a heretic. Error is (in part) a matter of the intellect whereas heresy is a matter of the *will*. Many Christians hold heretical opinions without even realizing it. They are not heretics. The heretic is a professed Christian who knows what the orthodox Christian view is and nevertheless *sets his or her will against it*. Gary Thorne writes, "The church must be inclusive of all those baptized who hold heretical opinions and views on their way to embrace the fuller truth of the gospel as found in the church. But the church cannot be inclusive of heretics."[9] This is because the heretic "by definition deliberately sets his will over against that of the church. Heretics want the body of Christ on their own terms, and to offer Eucharistic hospitality to

---

8. Arguably, the title "Lord" also alludes to the name of the God of Israel, Yhwh. Jews in this period (including Jesus and the authors of the NT) would never speak the name Yhwh but would substitute the word *kyrios* (Lord). The use of the title "Lord" for Jesus in the early church did draw on this connection with the divine name.

9. Thorne, "Heresy Excludes Itself" (2013), 25.

such persons is for the church to be complicit in the harm that will come to one who refuses to discern the Lord's body."[10] The church can be a very broad and inclusive body but it cannot be limitlessly broad without losing its gospel-grounded identity.

The Story in Modernity

Modernity was not kind to the story, which was subject to attacks from various quarters and became a source of embarrassment to many cultured Christians. Theologians knew that they needed to find ways to incorporate the insights of the new philosophies, the new sciences, and the new historical research but how to do that? Increasing numbers of theologians felt the pressure to deny literal miracles and to deny philosophically "implausible" (or even "impossible") claims such as the incarnation of the infinite God in finite human flesh or the idea that one God can be three persons. It is not hard to find theologians from the eighteenth century to the current day who have rejected key elements of the Nicene Creed in an attempt to make Christianity plausible to its "cultured despisers" in the modern world. *This* is the third schism.

It is *not* a question of any lack of integrity or bad motives on the part of Christians who have moved away from creedal orthodoxy. In most cases it has been born of a passionate desire to hold on to the faith in the midst of a radically new and challenging intellectual environment. The post-orthodox believers simply want to find ways of making the faith relevant in their day. However, our contention is that in pursuit of this noble goal the faith has sometimes been modified to such an extent that fundamental aspects of the core of the gospel story itself have been abandoned. What remains ceases to be in sufficient continuity with the apostolic Christian faith.

The Trinity and Chalcedonian Christology have been regularly subject to suspicion within certain parts of Protestantism. The seventeenth and eighteenth centuries saw a significant numbers of nonconformists (Presbyterians, Congregationalists, and Baptists) embracing Arianism (denial of the full divinity of Jesus) and unitarianism (denial of the Trinity). Interestingly such moves to embrace heresy were often made by Christians with a strong commitment to the final authority of the Bible in matters of faith and practice. But for them a key insight of the Reformation was a rejection of church tradition. It was tradition that had buried the pure gospel taught

10. Ibid.

by the apostles and it was the principled rejection of what was considered distorting human tradition that opened up the Bible to speak afresh. When the Bible was put into the hands of ordinary people and read in this way increasing numbers felt that the Bible did not really teach that God was triune or that Jesus was God. By the beginning of the nineteenth century in Britain the General Baptists, for instance, were largely unitarian. (For a contemporary example one need only think of Oneness Pentecostalism, which embraces Sabellianism—the heretical modalist belief that the one person of God manifests as three different personas—because it believes it to be more biblical than Trinitarianism.)

On top of the impact of the rejection by some believers of Christian tradition was the growing role of autonomous reason. Even very Bible-believing Christians in the eighteenth and nineteenth centuries felt a strong commitment to the deliverances of "reason." And many felt that traditional beliefs such as incarnation and Trinity were illogical and unreasonable. There was also a pietistic embrace of heart-felt religion and a worry that such abstract teachings as are found in the creeds seem remote from a passionate, lived Christian life. For Immanuel Kant "the doctrine of the Trinity provides nothing, absolutely nothing, of practical value, even if one claims to understand it."[11] It was, he thought, a "mere accidental addition" to Christianity. Thus, even the Protestant majority that still maintained traditional beliefs often pushed them to the periphery in practice, hidden away like embarrassing relatives. This only served to magnify the perception of their marginality and limited relevance. Thus modernity created the conditions in which a third schism could be opened up deep within the heart of the Protestant churches themselves. From there it spread eventually, though to a lesser degree, to Catholicism.

The rise of historical biblical criticism, especially in the nineteenth and twentieth centuries, raised new questions about the historical reliability of the Bible in general and the Gospels in particular. In light of the new Newtonian understanding of a mechanistic universe the miracles of Jesus were obvious candidates for suspicion—there are no interventions in the cause-and-effect chain of explanations for events in the world. There are no "gaps" in the chain where God "breaks in" to do miracles. This, of course, also meant no literal virgin birth and no literal resurrection. Now even many liberal-minded Christians often resisted such radical conclusions because they so obviously struck at the heart of Christian truth claims. Nevertheless,

11. Kant, *Der Streit der Fakultäten* (1917), 38–39.

those Christians who felt drawn by such scientific approaches were led to distance themselves more and more from the miraculous aspects of Christianity. Jesus began to be seen as a great moral teacher—the greatest such teacher there has been—rather than as a miracle-working God-man. The late nineteenth century was awash with such Jesuses.

The fortunes of traditional Christian faith within Protestantism have waxed and waned since the Enlightenment. And the rejection of creedal orthodoxy has taken various different forms. Sometimes it has been a simple rejection of such beliefs and a claim that Christianity can get by without them. At other times it has involved a radical reinterpretation of traditional beliefs such that they are invested with meanings previously unknown. For instance, Don Cupitt, in *Taking Leave of God* and *Creation out of Nothing*, argues that talk about God creating the world *ex nihilo* can still be helpful but only if understood to mean that humans, through creative use of language to redescribe the world, are able to bring order and goodness and meaning out of the meaningless chaos that the world is. *That* is what Cupitt (during that period of his philosophical development) meant by phrases like "God created the world." His work inspired the founding of The Sea of Faith Movement and there were infamous cases of Anglican vicars connected to the movement who were, in any usual understanding of the word, atheists and yet who had no qualms about reciting the Creed because what they meant by its different clauses was not what their congregations meant (nor what any Christians in the history of the church have meant). In this way they claimed to affirm the Creed while actually rejecting it.

A different though related danger has been a sophisticated relativization of creedal faith that allows the claims to be "true" but only relative to the socially-embedded conceptual systems of the particular faith community. So Jesus really is God and man *within the "language games" of orthodox Christianity*. To say that Jesus was no more than human is false *within those same language games*. It is said that we misunderstand such theological language if we suppose that it is making some metaphysically realist reference to a God "out there" beyond language. Outside the social framework of Christian worship and living the language about Jesus as the God-man is *neither true nor false*; it simply has no use. This analysis is not intended as a proposal for how Christian language *should* work but purports to be an account of how it does, and always has, actually functioned when being true to itself. Thus it is not intended as an attack on the Creed. Indeed, it is usually offered as a gift, aimed at helping Christians to better understand their own language, thereby avoiding the pitfalls of distorting it. This non-realist approach to Christian theological language is much more sophisticated than the crass and fuzzy all-religious-beliefs-are-true claims of some in modern pop culture. It reflects the application of some high-level, albeit very controversial, philosophy of language to theological speaking. Nevertheless, we believe that it represents a threat to creedal orthodoxy. The creeds were offered as metaphysically realist claims and have always been understood as such within orthodoxy. Their truth was not simply grounded in the language and praxis of the community but in the transcendent God. We believe that Christian theology bursts the bounds of anti-realist philosophies of language. For instance, the assertion that God created the universe *ex nihilo* (out of nothing) is the radical claim that everything in the universe depends upon God for its existence from moment to moment. God, on the other hand, depends upon nothing. This claim is unacceptably relativized if we also wish to say, even if in a different language game (e.g., a philosophy lecture as opposed to Christian worship), that God's reality is internal to language. Then God depends upon language speakers for his being and it is God, rather than the universe, that has been created. But Christians believe that God was there even when there were no people to speak about him.[12]

Why It Matters 1—Resurrection: A Case Study

Let's take a case study of how the pressures of modernity pose a challenge to orthodox faith. Christians confess of Jesus that "on the third day he was

---

12. Actually things are a little more complicated than this. Anti-realists would agree that claims such as "God is dependent on nothing for his existence" and "everything depends on God for its existence" are true within Christian language games. They would also agree that claims such as "God depends on language speakers for his reality" are necessarily false within such contexts. Further, they would possibly say that the utterance "God depends on language speakers for his reality" is not really an utterance that has any form of life in which it makes sense—outside of religious language games language about God normally has no function so such utterances are simply out of place, and hence misuses of language. Nevertheless, it remains the case that this philosophically controversial approach to language and truth does mean that without language speakers there is no truth about God. Christian theology asserts, to the contrary, that truth is ultimately grounded *in God*. If there is a word in the beginning it is the divine Word (John 1:1) and not the human word. The very claims of Christian theology itself resist the constraints of anti-realism. This is obviously an issue that requires considerable discussion but space prohibits.

raised from the dead," and of themselves a hope for "the resurrection of the dead." In the ancient world this very Jewish confession was somewhat scandalous because what resurrection meant was resurrection *of the body* and ancient views of the body were often less than positive (Acts 17:32). Bodies are changeable and get sick and old and die—they are at the opposite end of the spectrum from perfection. Thus many considered the body akin to a prison in which the soul was trapped and from which it longed to escape. For Christians to speak of the life of the age to come as an *embodied* life—albeit a radically transformed bodily life (1 Cor 15:36–49)—did not resonate with the spirit of the age and the social pressure was on the church to tone down that stupid claim. But the early Christian leaders were uncompromising. Even as the church sought to appropriate wisdom from Greek philosophical thought in expounding its biblical theology it was ever conscious that *the gospel* always took priority over the wisdom of Athens when matters of dogmatic truth were at stake. So when Greek thought ran counter to biblical theology it was modified. One such area was resurrection.

> In the end, *flesh.* That has been the conviction of the Church's best theologians, who in their eschatological imagination have dared to populate the coming world with living humans, that is, bodies fully alive, rejoined and renewed in the coming world. According to this vision, nothing is lost at the resurrection. On the day of Christ's return the saints are made new, yet in this newness everything is strangely familiar: muscle and bones, skin and scars, all beautiful, and altogether the persons who once lived. Bodies which grew and acted and sickened and died are somehow identical with the bodies raised by God on the last day. *Credo in resurrectionem carnis*, says the Apostles Creed, representative of this holy imagination: *I believe in the resurrection of the flesh.*[13]

Why did this matter so much to the church? Because they believed that matter mattered. Christians told a story in which God created *all* things—in all their physicality—and declared them all *good* (Gen 1) and in which the Son of God came "in the flesh" (John 1:14; 1 John 4:21; 2 John 7). There was no scope in that story for a negative view of materiality and embodied existence. To denigrate the body was to denigrate the God that made it and was incarnate in it. The resurrection of Jesus is therefore God's YES to the

---

13. Hitchcock, *Karl Barth and the Resurrection of the Flesh* (2013), 1.

physical; God's affirmation of the goodness of creation in all its fullness; God's eternal beatification of *space* and *time* and *matter*.

But in modernity belief in the resurrection of Jesus has become scandalous again. Not because of a philosophical commitment to negative views of matter, as in the ancient world, but because of a philosophical commitment to a view of the universe as a closed system with no interventions from outside the system. In such a universe it is hard to make sense of how a resurrection could actually happen.

Many Christians have been tempted to modify belief in the resurrection of Christ so that they can affirm that Christ was raised from the dead but deny that this was an event that took place in history, in space-time; to suggest that even if we found the tomb of Jesus with his bones still in it there would be no problem for faith because belief in the resurrection is not about what happened to the corpse of Jesus. The German theologian Rudolf Bultmann, whose theology was often deeply insightful, famously said that the resurrection of Jesus was not an event of past history ("An historical fact which involves a resurrection from the dead is utterly inconceivable!"[14]) but a mythical attempt to convey the meaning of the cross—to affirm "that his death was not just an ordinary human death, but the judgment and salvation of the world, depriving death of its power." The resurrection, in other words, is a mythic way of communicating the idea that the cross (which *was* an event in history) has transformative significance: "faith in the resurrection is really the same thing as faith in the saving efficacy of the cross." Bultmann argues that the resurrection is first and foremost an "eschatological event" (and no mere animation of a corpse) that is brought into the present lived experience of believers in the preaching of the gospel and the response of faith. "If the event of Easter Day is in any sense an historical event additional to the event of the cross, it is nothing else than the rise of faith in the risen Lord." Preaching the gospel word and faith in the resurrection *is* the resurrection made present in the now. That new existential stance toward life on the part of the disciples *was* the resurrection of Christ, *was* Christ living in them. Following in Bultmann's footsteps, David Jenkins, former Bishop of Durham, infamously expressed agnosticism and indifference about whether the empty tomb was a historical fact.

Rev. David Jennings, Canon Theologian at Leicester Cathedral, wants to allow the diversity of Christian interpretations of the resurrection to

---

14. All Bultmann quotations are taken from "New Testament and Mythology" (1953), 38–43.

include the denial of its historicity so long as we affirm that "something significant happened which was of life-changing proportions."[15] Jennings is keen that his minimalist version of resurrection should be allowed to count as permissible Christian alternative in order to avoid the Church of England becoming a sect! A claim that echoes David Boulton's comment in 1999 that clergy that are Sea of Faith members—many of whom were atheists—wish to remain as clergy within the Church of England because they "refuse to abandon it to fundamentalists."[16] (But since when has believing in God been fundamentalist? Since when has insisting on the bodily resurrection been sectarian?)

Whether Jennings's minimalism is consistent with Christian faith very much depends on what he means by denying that the resurrection was an historical fact. His article is less than clear. He rightly points out that in the NT accounts "something else is going on than *just* the recording of an historical event" (italics mine). Indeed. He also rightly points out that the resurrection is not historical *in the same way* that the Battle of Hastings in 1066 is historical. It is an *eschatological* event (as Bultmann rightly stressed) and thus not "historical" in any mundane way, not merely another event alongside others. That is fine as far as it goes but it is too vague. Christians do, of course, believe that something life-changing happened at the resurrection but such a minimalist assertion is not adequate to count as faith in the resurrection. Even an atheist could be prepared to assert that much. And the fact that the resurrection is an eschatological event does not mean that it is not something that happened to Jesus' *body*. On the contrary, it is an eschatological transformation of the embodied Jesus.

The problem with all these approaches is that they are radical changes of the meaning of the word "resurrection" as it has operated within Christian faith. Resurrection, from day one, meant resurrection *of the body*. It was not that the early Christians, being old-world people, could not imagine any form of afterlife without reanimated bodies—there were plenty of paradigms in the ancient world for non-physical future life. They could easily imagine non-embodied afterlives but they confessed not the mere postmortem existence of Jesus (as a spirit or as hope in his followers' hearts or whatever) but his *resurrection*. And to deny a bodily resurrection or an empty tomb *is* to deny resurrection.

15. http://www.cathedral.leicester.anglican.org/Highlights/documents/David JenningsBlog.pdf.

16. http://news.bbc.co.uk/1/hi/uk/393479.stm.

Should this worry us? Yes. The early church fought hard to maintain a positive embracing of embodied life and belief in resurrection was a key part of that. The problem with denying bodily resurrection is that one is in danger of undermining Christian commitment to the goodness and *eternal value* of space, time, and the physical world. Resurrection offers a Christian valuation of the goodness of the body (for our beautiful future is an embodied future) but also a recognition of its current flaws (for our bodies now are indeed weak and broken and eventually grow old and die). We learn to accept the limitations but to hope for healing.

Why It Matters 2—A Case Study: Pluralism

A second area in which modern Christians are tempted to a rejection of orthodoxy is in the area of religious pluralism. More than in any previous age modern people are aware of the rich diversity of faiths—indeed, most people in urban areas will interact with people of various faiths on a day-to-day basis. With growing exposure has come a growing understanding of different religious traditions and a growing respect for their adherents. For Christians this has presented a challenge. The church has always claimed that Jesus is absolutely unique—he alone is God incarnate and it is through him alone that salvation comes to creation. But such exclusive claims increasingly appear very arrogant and inappropriate.

Some Christians, feeling uncomfortable with these traditional claims of the church and with attempts to convert others to Christianity, have developed pluralist theologies that aspire to be more "open." Pluralist theologies are not all the same but at their heart they seek to find ways to affirm the equal validity of all religious traditions. Christian faith is, as such, no better or truer than any other faith.

Let us briefly consider one classic example of pluralism—that of the Christian philosopher John Hick. Hick's version of pluralism begins by placing the "infinite Real" (Hick's preferred term for God) beyond the scope of any human concepts. Different religious traditions all conceive of, experience, and respond to this same ineffable reality in very different, culturally conditioned ways. Each religion in its own ways enables the transformation of human beings from being self-centered to being Reality-centered. Each religion thus provides "alternative soteriological 'spaces' within which, or 'ways' along which, men and women can find salvation/liberation/ultimate fulfillment."[17] Arrogance in relation to those of other faiths is out of place because no faith is truer than another.

Hick realizes that traditional Christian orthodoxy presents a problem: "If Jesus was God incarnate, the Christian religion is unique in having been founded by God in person. The Christian story is that in Jesus God came down to earth and inaugurated a new and redeemed community, the church; and it seems self-evident that God must wish all human creatures to become part of this community; so the church is called to convert the human race to the Christian faith."[18]

Hick's solution is to reject the Christology of the Creed. He argues (a) that the historical Jesus did not see himself as God incarnate; (b) the traditional claim that Jesus is fully divine and fully human is logically impossible; and (c) that it leads to an anti-pluralist faith and practice with harmful consequences. Hick proposes instead that we understand the incarnation as a myth or a metaphor: "[W]e see in Jesus a human being extraordinarily open to God's influence and thus living to an extraordinary extent as God's agent on earth, 'incarnating' the divine purpose for human life."[19] This creates the space for his pluralist theology to operate.

Now it is impossible to adequately explain or evaluate Hick's complex thought here, but we will make a few brief comments.[20] Hick's theology is thoroughly modernist, drawing explicitly on the stark and unbridgeable distinction that Immanuel Kant drew between things *in themselves* (which are utterly unknowable) and things *as they appear to us*. God (the Real) is utterly unknowable in itself but we can know it *as it appears to us* in our different, culturally and religiously diverse contexts. Hick's approach, of course, depends on different religious traditions accepting this Kantian distinction and agreeing to his assertion that their own understandings of the religious ultimate are no more correct as representations of the Real than those of others. But few religious believers would be content with that! Typically, while most religious traditions happily admit—nay, insist on—the inadequacy of their understandings of the Ultimate Reality they are unlikely to accept that any understanding is as good as any other. Take the Trinity, for instance. To accept Hick's view would require Christians to

17. Hick, *Interpretation of Religion* (1989), 240.

18. Hick, *Metaphor of God Incarnate* (1993), 87.

19. Ibid., 12.

20. For evaluations, see, for instance, Sinkinson, *The Universe of Faiths* (2001); Nah, *Christian Theology and Religious Pluralism* (2012).

believe that the Muslim's denial of God's triunity is *just as true* as their own affirmation of it. It would also require Muslims to accept that while their fervent denial of the Trinity is correct *so too* is the Christian assertion that God is Father, Son, and Spirit. But this can only happen if both faiths accept that their beliefs about God are not really beliefs about God-in-Godself but only beliefs about how God appears to them; in other words, that their beliefs about God tell us *absolutely nothing* about God/the Real as such.

Christian orthodoxy has always understood its beliefs about God and Jesus to open us up to both the truth and the mystery of God. Its claims about the Trinity and the incarnation have always been taken as telling us *something* fundamental and true—albeit simultaneously beyond our rational comprehension—about what God is in Godself. Hick's pluralism works by denying this. But if pluralism requires the rejection of the Trinity and of creedal understandings of Jesus then so much the worse for pluralism!

Hick is correct that orthodox incarnational theology *does* hold that the revelation of God in Jesus is unique—both unsurpassed and unsurpassable. He is also correct that orthodoxy does see the salvation of the world as essentially bound up with what God did in Jesus. And so he is right that Christian orthodoxy *cannot* see all religions as *equally* true. (Of course, this is not simply a feature of Christianity—traditional Islam or Buddhism, say, would similarly reject the notion that everyone is equally right.)

However, we do need to point out that Christian orthodoxy has the capacity for far more generosity to the religious other than is often imagined. Christianity can very happily acknowledge that there is genuine divine revelation in non-Christian faiths (as well as error). Similarly, orthodoxy can affirm that non-Christian people can have real and transformative encounters with the true God and can be genuinely good and righteous people. Furthermore, Christianity can be fully supportive of inter-faith dialogue aimed at mutual understanding and respect, and Christians can happily be open to learning new things about walking in God's ways from people of non-Christian faiths. On top of that, orthodox Christianity is compatible with the claim that people outside of the church can be saved through Christ (a view known as inclusivism).

Of course, this will not satisfy pluralists because it still evaluates the truth, goodness, and beauty (and the error, badness, and ugliness) in non-Christian faiths (and the church) from the perspective of Christian faith as the standard. So be it. That is what it *means* to accept the truth of Christianity.[21]

Why It Matters 3—Christology: A Case Study

Finally, we should consider contemporary challenges to orthodox teaching on Jesus. The Council of Chalcedon (451) expressed the balance that the church sought to achieve:

> We, then, following the holy Fathers, all with one consent, teach people to confess one and the same Son, our Lord Jesus Christ, the same perfect in Godhead and also perfect in manhood; truly God and truly man, of a reasonable [rational] soul and body; consubstantial [co-essential] with the Father according to the Godhead, and consubstantial with us according to the Manhood; in all things like unto us, without sin; begotten before all ages of the Father according to the Godhead, and in these latter days, for us and for our salvation, born of the Virgin Mary, the Mother of God, according to the Manhood; one and the same Christ, Son, Lord, only begotten, to be acknowledged in two natures, inconfusedly, unchangeably, indivisibly, inseparably; the distinction of natures being by no means taken away by the union, but rather the property of each nature being preserved, and concurring in one Person (*prosopon*) and one Subsistence (*hypostasis*), not parted or divided into two persons, but one and the same Son, and only begotten God, the Word, the Lord Jesus Christ; as the prophets from the beginning [have declared] concerning Him, and the Lord Jesus Christ Himself has taught us, and the Creed of the holy Fathers has handed down to us.

This dense but carefully balanced statement—the fruit of four centuries of Christian experience and reflection—seeks to hold together the full divinity and full humanity of the one person of Christ. There have always been many alternative versions of Jesus but we shall focus on one contemporary example, that of New Testament scholar Marcus Borg. Borg

21. And in this regard pluralism cannot claim the high ground, for it too evaluates all religions beliefs from its own privileged perspective, its own claims to understand the overarching truth of the situation—a truth predicated on modern Western philosophical assumptions and beliefs. Religious ideas that do not conform to this modern Western vision—such as traditional Christology—are *rejected as false*. So the generosity of pluralism is arguably not as generous as it appears.

is an interesting case study because he writes from within the church (he is Canon Theologian at Trinity Cathedral in Portland, OR), because he is existentially committed to the truth of God he sees in Jesus and wants to find new ways of affirming traditional formulations of Christian faith in the modern world, and because he is very influential among "progressive" and "emerging" Christians.[22]

Borg is best known as a relatively liberal historical Jesus scholar. Jesus, says Borg, should be understood in his first-century context as a Jewish mystic with a profound sense of his own encounter with and relationship to Yhwh, a prophet to Israel, a wisdom teacher, a healer and exorcist, and a non-violent opponent to the domination system of Roman imperialism. Neither Jesus himself nor any of his contemporaries considered him to be divine. The pre-Easter Jesus (the "historical Jesus"), in other words, was a Spirit-filled prophet *but was not God*. However, the post-Easter Jesus (i.e., Jesus as existentially experienced by believers as an ongoing presence since his crucifixion[23]) "is a divine reality—is indeed one with God."[24] The community experienced Jesus to be a divine light in the world, a source of spiritual life, a path out of darkness, and so began to speak of him in very exalted terms to communicate this reality. The language of the Creed is simply a development of this tradition but should be interpreted metaphorically and parabolically, not metaphysically. Borg himself has no qualms about reciting the Creed so long as he can interpret it as a culturally and historically situated expression of the church's experience of Jesus expressed in devotional and metaphorical language.

Borg also affirms that there is even a sense in which the pre-Easter Jesus (the historical Jesus) is "the embodiment or incarnation of God."[25] His relationship with God was so deep that his disciples past and present can see God's character, passion, and vision embodied in his life and teachings. In him Christians see what God is like—he mediates the sacred to his followers like an icon and in a poetic sense can be seen as God enfleshed. He

---

22. Borg's christological proposals are not new but represent a contemporary version of some ideas in liberal nineteenth- and twentieth-century biblical and theological scholarship.

23. Borg, like Bultmann, does not believe in an empty tomb and a bodily resurrection of Jesus but he claims that this does not make the resurrection less true or less real. The truth of the resurrection is akin to that of a parable—it speaks of God's Yes to Jesus and his No to the empire that unjustly killed him (Borg, *Jesus* [2011], chap. 10).

24. Borg and Wright, *Meaning of Jesus* (1999), 146.

25. Ibid.

is *for Christians* the decisive revelation of God (which is *not* to say the only, or only adequate, revelation of God). For Borg, "to be Christian is to affirm, 'Here, in Jesus, I see more clearly than anywhere else what God is like.'"[26]

Finally, we should note that Borg does not see the historical Jesus as the "real" Jesus and the post-Easter Jesus as somehow less real. The real Jesus includes *both* the pre-Easter *and* the post-Easter Jesus. The *real* Jesus is Jesus as he was in history *and* as subsequently experienced and understood by believers; in other words, for Borg the real Jesus is the Jesus we find in the New Testament, rather merely than a historical reconstruction of the man from Galilee.[27]

Borg is interesting because he writes with passion as one who finds God in Jesus and who seeks to follow in the way. His vision can seem very attractive as a way of seeking to embrace modernity and the Christian encounter with Christ. Indeed, orthodox Christians can affirm large amounts of what he writes about Jesus and he has much to contribute to the church's understanding of her Lord. *Yet* his Christology clearly departs radically from that of historic Christianity.

It seems to us that Borg's claims about Jesus bear an interesting resemblance to an early Christian heresy known as adoptionism. Classical adoptionists believed that Jesus was an ordinary human being but that at his baptism the Christ/Spirit came upon him and from that point he was adopted by God as the Son. At this point he became divine in some sense (though not equal with the Father). Borg's view is not exactly the same but he too affirms that Jesus was an ordinary human being who at some point encountered God in mystical intimacy and was so filled with the divine Spirit that he became a vehicle of divine. He understands all the language about Jesus' divinity to be a poetic way of making the point that we can discover what God is like by looking at and listening to Jesus, the parable of God *par excellence*.

This, however, is to deny what the church has always claimed—that Jesus was *literally* the divine Logos made flesh, and that as the divine Logos he was *literally* pre-existent and *literally* the one through whom the Father created all things (John 1:1–18). If these claims are true of Jesus then they do not merely *become* "true" of the Post-Easter Jesus. Indeed, if they are true of the post-Easter Jesus then they *must* be true of the pre-Easter Jesus (and if they are not true of the pre-Easter Jesus then they *cannot* be true

26. Ibid., 156.

27. Borg, *Jesus* (2011), 304.

94

of the post-Easter Jesus). One cannot *become* the one through whom God created the universe. One either is or one is not. Jesus may well have been a man in whom we find God but that in and of itself could not make him the Creator nor could it make him "of one substance with the Father." He may be filled with God and he may be a window on God but on Borg's view he cannot be the second person of the Trinity made flesh. (It should go without saying that we are not suggesting that people during Jesus' earthly ministry understood him in these ways—they certainly did not. The understanding of who Jesus was developed gradually through Jesus' ministry and after his resurrection.)

Borg, of course, knows this and so reinterprets the traditional theological claims in poetic, non-literal ways. But can the traditional claims about Jesus sustain such an interpretation? For instance, Borg says that being the creator is "true" of the Christ of faith but not the Christ of history.[28] But *in what sense* could talk of Jesus as the one through whom God created the world be true *if Jesus was not the one through whom God created the world?* Even if one wants to find a mythical way of saying how much Jesus means to us, calling him the creator of the universe is a very odd way to do that! And if Jesus is not "of one substance with the Father," calling him such and worshiping him alongside the Father goes far beyond the kind of recognition even Borg's Jesus warrants. It falls into idolatry. It seems to us that one cannot do justice to the New Testament testimony about Jesus' identity if it is translated into claims about how we see what God is like by looking at Jesus. As the early church realized, we need to go beyond metaphor to metaphysics to do justice to the language.

Borg's Jesus is not fully God and fully human; rather, he is the ultimate Spirit-filled man. The question then is whether the early church was right to insist on a Jesus who is both fully human *and fully divine.* For orthodoxy the full divinity of Christ is important not merely to do justice to claims made by certain New Testament texts and early Christian practices (such as the worship of Jesus)—though it is certainly that—but also because it was felt that if Jesus is to be the ultimate revelation of God then while he must be *fully* human he cannot be *merely* human. In John's Gospel, for instance, the reason that Jesus is the unsurpassed and unsurpassable revelation of God is because he has come down from above (3:11–13). He alone, as the Logos who was with God and was God, has seen the Father and can reveal him (1:1–2, 18). God can, of course, reveal himself in many and various

28. Ibid., 109.

ways through prophets but the divine self-revelation is of a different order because Jesus is more than a prophet—he is the divine Son through whom God made all things, "the radiance of God's glory and the exact representation of his being" (Heb 1:1–3).

The church also claimed that if Jesus is to be the savior, the one through whom God reconciles the world to himself, he has to be both fully human (to save *us*) and fully divine (to *save* us). If he is to be the perfect mediator between God and humanity he has to be human (to represent us before God) and divine (to represent God before us). This claim was spelled out in different ways by different thinkers depending on how salvation was pictured but the common core was that only God can save us and for Jesus to save us he had to be more than a Spirit-filled man. The orthodox Jesus is Emmanuel—*God himself* with us; Borg's Jesus is not.

Conclusion

Oliver Quick is absolutely right when he says, "The real and permanent object of Christian faith is not the creeds but Christ and his gospel."[29] This is true, importantly true. We are saved by grace, not theology; by Christ, not doctrine. Nevertheless, through the Creed the Spirit continues to bear authoritative witness to Christ—to who he is and what he has done and will do. The narrative they testify to and interpret *is* Christian belief. This *is* the old, old story. If this story comes apart, then Christianity comes apart.

29. Quick, *Doctrines of the Creed* (1971), 18.

6

Deep Worship

Orthodoxia *as Right Worship*

> Great art thou, O Lord, and greatly to be praised. . . . And man
> desires to praise thee, for he is part of thy creation. . . . Thou hast
> prompted him, that he should delight to praise thee, for thou hast
> made us for thyself and restless is our heart until it comes to rest
> in thee.[1]

Christian Worship in Consumer Culture

MAKING CHRISTIAN WORSHIP GATHERING culturally relevant is a worthy
endeavor and one that Christians across the generations have engaged
in, in many and various ways. Such contextualization is essential but also
brings inherent risks. The danger is that it may be that some of the features
of a particular culture that we seek to bring to church in the pursuit of
relevance are actually subtly undermining authentic Christian worship. We
need discernment.

Take the entertainment culture of the modern West as an example.
We are all consumers now and we are used to being regularly stimulated
and entertained as we pursue the next shot in the arm. Combine this with
the new social location of churches as voluntary clubs existing in the private sphere alongside other leisure activities. Church, in the minds of many
people, exists as a form of "leisure" activity for old people and weirdos. If

---

1. Augustine, *Conf.* 1.1.

we are to pull in the punters we need to be hip-hop rather than hip-op—we need to be entertaining. But while there are opportunities here there are also dragons lurking nearby. If we position worship as a form of Christian entertainment we will shape Christians who consume worship as a product; Christians that move from one worship "high" to the next, chasing one stimulating event after another; Christians that assess how good the worship was by how fuzzy it made them feel; and Christians that will leave one congregation for another with little hesitation if a more entertaining gathering springs up in another church. But this kind of worship is, at rock bottom, all about *me*, and God is approached as if he were under some obligation to keep me happy. He is my drug of choice, but if he gets boring I'll move on.

And if you don't think that worship is being transformed into a consumer product just consider the relatively big business of selling worship music and marketing large worship concerts. Increasingly the advertising promises life-changing experiences for those who buy in, that we'll be swept into God's presence, that we'll never be the same again. Of course, the reality always falls short but it's good enough to make us chase the next big thing. Remember, entertainment as a format is not neutral but conditions us to want more of the same.

And making worship entertaining does draw crowds—it works. At least, it works if we think that big numbers of people feeling good for a while is the goal. But do we have a congregation or an audience? Do we have worship or a performance? Are we forming disciples or keeping our customers happy? Are we honoring God or pleasing ourselves?

Please do not mishear what we are saying. The dangers of consumer worship are created to a large extent by the new cultural frame within which the church is located. Whether we like it or not people—Christian and non-Christian—will, to one degree or another, approach church as a leisure activity. And that is the case for any form of public worship, traditional or modern. The question is how much we accommodate that orientation and how much we seek to resist and reshape it. We are not suggesting for one moment that we make worship gatherings as dull as possible simply to stop people treating them as a form of fun! God forbid! The tradition has never been averse to beautiful and joyful worship. What we are saying is that if we are to be true to the aspirations of the tradition the agenda for worship has to be determined by *the gospel*, not entertainment culture. And aspirations is the right word here. Throughout history Christian worship has regularly fallen short of its ideals but the key thing is that *it had ideals*; it had a target. As the old proverb says, you have to aim at the moon to hit the mountaintop; aim at nothing and you are sure to hit it. In this chapter we wish to look at some of the aspects of the ideals of worship as understood within the tradition.

Ortho-Doxia: Now and Not Yet

We need to understand *ortho-doxia*, rightly aligned worship, in a twofold way. In one sense, orthodox worship is a simple binary: worship is *either* orthodox *or* it is not; it is authentic worship *or* it is not. Worship aims to bring an acceptable offering to God, but how can we, broken people that we are, bring a gift that is fitting for the Holy One? How can we offer acceptable worship? The answer is that we can do so because of our mediator, Jesus. The chief worshiper of the Father is the God-man himself, Jesus the Messiah (Heb 2:12). He offers *ortho-doxia* to God as our human representative. And Christian worship is worship that is offered to God in and through Christ by those who are united to him by the Spirit through faith. Our imperfect worship passes, as it were, through the filter of Christ's own perfect worship and is thereby purified. But worship offered in our own name rather than that of Christ will not be filtered and will contain all the impurities we bring. Thus it will not be "rightly aligned." So first and foremost orthodox worship is worship offered to the Father, *through* the Son, *in* the Spirit. If it is, then it brings "right glory" because Christ's worship does.

But, in another sense, authentic Christian worship is not a simple binary: not *either* on *or* off. There is a process of sanctification involved, a journey of transformation, as our devotion is changed "from one degree of glory to another." The Holy Spirit leads us—both as communities and as individuals—on a voyage, teaching us how to become in our own experienced reality what we already are in Christ. And here *ortho-doxia* is like the water flowing from a tap: it can be dripping, dribbling, flowing, gushing, or pounding. In experienced reality our worship is right to the extent it is conformed to the image of Christ. So orthodox, from this angle, is not so much what we *are* as what we are *becoming*; not so much where we are *at* as where we are *heading*. It is an eschatological feast that can be tasted in present reality.

So as we travel this road, in Christ and assisted by the Spirit, it is helpful to get a sense of some of the features of worship that is rightly aligned.

Ortho-Doxia: The Ideal

Ortho-Doxia *Is God-focused*

One interesting observation on human psychology is that when we focus exclusively on ourselves and make the pursuit of our own happiness our life-project we often find that although happiness always seems within reach, like the end of the rainbow, it ever eludes us. But when we turn our gaze outwards toward others we discover that joy finds us, when we are not even looking for it.

There is something of this dynamic in worship. There are, in fact, many benefits for us in worship. We can find love, joy, peace, healing, restoration, and a sense of belonging. We can find rest for our restless hearts. Worship is spiritual formation and it is good for us. However, if we are engaging in worship primarily in order to gain these benefits for ourselves then we will find them in small measure. The more we move our focus away from ourselves toward God, giving him honor whether we get anything from it or not, the more we find that our cup runs over with the wine of divine blessing. Joy is found when we stop pursuing joy and start pursuing God.

Giving glory to God for God's sake, whether or not he blesses us, can seem a very pointless motivation to many people. Our culture is one that runs on functional logic and taking aside time to do stuff with no clear outcome seems an inefficient use of time. Why pray? You'd be better off doing something useful. But such extravagant "time-wasting" in the presence of God is at the heart of the loving devotion to which we are called—this crazy Godward orientation of the self. Marva Dawn provocatively speaks of worship as "a royal 'waste' of time."[2] Quite right! A glorious, counter-cultural waste of time!

We are not suggesting that the pleasure of worship is something to be avoided in pursuit of some Stoic detachment—far from it! Saint Augustine, to take one major voice from the tradition, is quite clear that human life finds its fulfillment in the enjoyment of God; the great saints often speak of the rapturous joy of knowing God. One might even speak of this, somewhat provocatively, as Christian hedonism. Our point is simply that the pleasure comes when we are not focusing on *it* but on *God*. It is in losing ourselves that we find ourselves.

---

2. See Dawn, *A Royal "Waste" of Time* (1999).

We are also not suggesting that there is no place for introspection in worship. On the contrary, to focus on God usually requires that we deal with issues where we are—there are worries that need to be brought before God and laid down, intercessions that need to be made, and sins that need to be acknowledged and dealt with. Worship is relationship and so such matters are important, but all of these issues find their "resolution" as we are enabled by God's grace to look away from ourselves—our worries, our circumstances, our sins, our sorrows—and fix our eyes upon God.

The great liturgies of the past were all designed to draw the attention of the worshipers toward God. The same can be said of the hymnic tradition. And they do draw attention to our sins and our needs but not so that our focus remains there. Instead they direct us to look to the Lord and to leave such matters at his feet.

One of the dangers with any form of Christian devotion in whatever tradition is that the music, the prayers, the buildings, the sermons, the icons, the rituals, which are all valuable because they serve as signs that *point beyond themselves to the divine*, become the focus of our attention. And the extent to which they do is the extent to which an act of worship is no longer occurring. Consider a Gregorian chant. At first it is not art at all—it is a heightened form of prayer. Not that it does not have aesthetic aspects, but those dimensions do not draw attention to themselves for their own sake but are aids for prayer. Now the chant can also be viewed at a level of abstraction, as something that helps us reflect on our mortality and God. Here it is not prayer as such but is still located in the God-directed life. However, the chant can suffer a second level of abstraction where it simply becomes a beautiful sound, art for art's sake, a concert to attend, and, with the advent of musical consumption by individuals in their own homes, it can eventually become just background musical wallpaper. When the Gregorian chant draws attention to itself as an artifact it is in danger of losing its soul. The many aspects of worship are like a window looking out across a beautiful vista. The window is not intended to be the focus of our attention; we are supposed to look *through* and not *at* it.

Of course, in the case of God things are not quite so simple. Perceiving God by means of the sights and sounds and touch and taste and smell of worship is something we must learn. And, as with learning a language, it can take lots of time and practice. When we learn a language we need to think very carefully about most of what we say. Our focus is on getting the words right and inflecting them properly. It is clumsy and stuttering and we make mistakes. But as time goes on the new language become easier and easier until it is second nature and we are no longer thinking *about* the language but thinking and communicating *through* the language. Language itself becomes, as it were, invisible, even though without it there would be no thought or communication at all.

Ortho-Doxia *Is Gospel-Shaped*

Christians are gospel people and the gospel story determines the shape of Christian worship. Indeed, the key criterion of whether worship is Christian is whether it is Christ-centered. Here the tradition offers a wealth of possibilities.

Gospel in Word

The great liturgies of the church are all Christocentric. They contain countless manifestations of the gospel in word: gospel-shaped prayers of all shapes and sizes, songs celebrating the evangel, readings from the Four Gospels, and sermons that expound on the good news. You cannot get away from the core message: "Jesus the Messiah died for our sins, was raised from the dead, and ascended to reign at God's right hand. Bow your knee and acknowledge him as Lord of creation."

Gospel in Sacrament

The gospel also informs the shape of the sacraments of the church. Let's take the two sacraments instituted by Jesus himself—baptism and Eucharist.

In baptism the narrative of an individual person's life is united by the Holy Spirit to the narrative of Christ. In its original form of immersion in water, a form still found in many churches, the person symbolically enacts the death, burial, and resurrection of Christ. They die with Christ, are buried with him in the water, and are raised up to new life (Rom 6). In the early church baptismal candidates would symbolically remove their clothing before entering the water and would put on new white clothes upon leaving it, representing stripping off their old self and being clothed with the new life of Jesus. In this way the candidates are saying that the cruciform pattern of Jesus' life—suffering and self-giving, followed by glory—will be what characterizes their own lives.

Eucharist too is fundamentally tied to the story of Jesus and his blood shed for us, his body broken for us. When we partake in the Lord's Supper we proclaim his death until he comes. And to consume the bread and wine is to ritually take the eternal life of Christ into our own lives. These two central rites reinforce the point that entry into the church and ongoing life within the church are grounded upon the good news.

The esteem for these sacraments in the tradition serves to keep the church centered on the good news. One danger of their marginalization in certain significant sections of evangelicalism (which, based on the cultural model of the pop concert, increasingly make singing choruses the paradigmatic center of Christian worship) is that we can lose sight of the story that makes us who we are.

Gospel in Time

The tradition also brings time itself into submission to Jesus. This comes across in various ways. It is not simply that the birth of Jesus becomes the fulcrum around which years are dated (BC and AD). Every week begins with worship on a Sunday, the day of Jesus' resurrection. According to Genesis 1, Sunday was the first day of creation, but in the New Testament it now becomes the first day of *new* creation.

> And we assemble together on Sunday, because it is the first day, on which God transformed darkness and matter, and made the world; and Jesus Christ our Savior rose from the dead on that day; for they crucified him the day before Saturday; and the day after Saturday, which is Sunday, he appeared to his apostles and disciples, and taught them these things which we have presented to you also for your consideration. (Justin Martyr *1 Apol.* 67)

So while Christians can meet to worship on other days this day has always held a special significance for the church. It is a weekly celebration of resurrection breaking into our age. (Some in the emerging church movement have advocated avoiding Sunday meetings so as to be "less religious." While such a move can have a place as a prophetic statement in certain circumstances it is in danger of losing more than is gained.)

Not simply dates and weeks but the worshipful rhythms of each year are determined by the narrative of the Messiah—Advent, Christmas, Epiphany, Lent, Easter, Pentecost. On top of that, the temporal progression through a liturgy, particularly eucharistic liturgies, move the congregation gradually toward the encounter with Christ in the feast. In all these ways worship redefines our relationship with time in "evangelical" ways. Modernity homogenizes time—all time is clock-time marching relentlessly forward—and so the tradition offers us a radically alternative way of being.

GOSPEL IN SPACE

By "gospel in space" we refer not to some science fiction story about evangelizing Martians. We speak instead of the way that the tradition found different ways of utilizing space in worship in Jesus-determined ways.

One might think in the first instance of the architecture of traditional church buildings. Now this varies from one tradition to another, from one country to another, and from one time period to another, but, whatever the variations, traditional church buildings (unlike the soulless warehouses of modern mega churches) are not merely functional boxes in which people can gather; they are theology written in stone, wood, glass, metal, and brick. Here there are volumes that could be written, but simply consider just two blindingly obvious examples: the classic shape of the Western cathedral and church is that of a cross. When Christians gather to worship they are gathering inside a huge cross! You can't get much more blatant than that!

Many Eastern church buildings are rectangular to symbolize the church as the ark of salvation (akin to Noah's ark) within which people are saved. This is sometimes combined in larger church buildings with a cross shape. The roof is usually domed, symbolizing heaven, and one will often see an image of Christ as *pantokrator*, ruler of the universe, in the dome. The sanctuary (the most holy place)—in which the altar, the Bible, and the eucharistic elements are kept—is hidden from the sight of the people for much of the act of worship by means of the iconostasis, a large screen covered in icons. This symbolism is used to great effect in the drama of the Divine Liturgy during which the clergy and deacons move back and forth through the doors in the iconostasis, entering heaven itself and bringing the body of Christ out for the people so that they may have life.

In Orthodox worship ritual space and time serve in the representation of the gospel:

> In the Divine Liturgy, everyone and everything is an image of something: the church building represents the space of the Kingdom of God, with Christ the King surrounded by the saints. The bishop represents Christ seated on the throne, as he will be in his

Kingdom. The priests represent the apostles who surround the bishop Christ on the *synthronon* [a raised seat in the apse with places for the bishop and priests]. The deacons represent the angels who . . . move between the people and the clergy. The people gathered together in one place and bringing the gifts (bread, wine, oil, etc.) express the scattered people of God, which in the Kingdom will come around Christ and, as the crown of creation, will bring with them the whole of the material world to be sanctified and saved as well. And all this iconic symbolism is not a static tableau but a movement in time, containing within it the historical time of salvation. Thus the bishop as another Christ does not simply sit on the throne; he *comes*. His entrance into the church is a great liturgical event . . . because it images the coming of Christ into the world at both his first and his Second Coming, and his reception by the clergy and people at the entrance of the church is the reception of Christ. . . . After the readings and the closing of the doors once the catechumens withdraw, everything from then on images future events in the Kingdom[3]

Now it is not the case that public worship has to include *this* liturgy, *that* kind of architecture, *those* annual festivals, and particular styles of preaching in order to be gospel-shaped. There is plenty of scope for innovation and living traditions have to be open to change across time and culture. But the historic worship of the church at very least presents us with rich models of how it can be done, models that serve as a resource for us.

Ortho-Doxia *Is Trinitarian*

Basil of Caesarea wrote, "[A]s we are baptized [i.e., in the name of the Father, of the Son, and of the Holy Spirit], so also do we believe; as we believe, so also do we recite the doxology" (*ep.* 159). Christian worship is not directed to some generic God; it is about the God revealed in the person of Christ—the Triune God. As such Christian worship has a Trinitarian shape. It has this in two ways. First, Christian worship is Trinitarian in its very dynamic. In prayer and praise we approach the Father, through the Son, in the Spirit (Eph 2:18). Our response to God is acceptable because it is a "gifted response" enabled by God himself. We have spoken of this aspect already above.

---

3. Zizioulas, "Symbolism and Realism in Orthodox Worship" (2011), 93.

Second, Christian worship is Trinitarian in its focus—we give "glory *to* the Father *and* to the Son *and* *to* the Holy Spirit." We offer adoration to the three persons of the Trinity. Of course, this Trinitarian balance can easily be lost. Often the Spirit disappears off the radar (even in Pentecostal worship), and in some evangelical groups everything seems to be Jesus-only worship, the irony being that by neglecting the Father such worship actually dishonors the Son who came to lead us to the Father.

> Christian worship should seek to bring God's church into a dynamic encounter with the Christian God—the Holy Trinity. It will ceaselessly and effortlessly move back and forth between the threeness of God and the unity of God. It will shift focus from Father, to Son, to Spirit and back again in a restless celebration of divine love and mystery. It will also highlight the perichoretic relations within the Godhead by not allowing the worshipers to lose sight of any of the Persons. At times the worship will draw the Father into focus however the Son and Spirit will be there, out of focus but still in our field of awareness. Other times the Son will attract our attention but not in such a way that we do not see Father and Spirit. When the Spirit attracts our worshiping attention it will always be as the Spirit of the Father and the Spirit of the Son. Worship that makes us aware of the inter-relationships within God is fully Trinitarian worship. Trinitarian worship is always "through the Son" and "in the Spirit" but is woven from an ever-changing mosaic of songs, prayers, Bible readings, testimonies, Spirit-gifts, sermons, Holy Communion, drama, dance, art, and more besides. The variety is endless and the possibilities infinite but at the heart of it all stands the mystery of the Holy Trinity. That is what Christian worship *is*.[4]

Ortho-Doxia *Is Existentially Engaged*

Right worship is not simply "going through the motions" or merely "saying the words," and it is not a spectator sport. Rather it is an existentially engaged encounter with God.

Some Christians have a suspicion that written prayers—which have played an important role in the tradition—have a tendency toward lifelessness, toward "dead religion." Now of course liturgy can be simply performed without faith or life—no doubt about it—but informal prayer can also be

4. Parry, *Worshiping Trinity* (2012), 167.

just as lifeless. There is a major misunderstanding here that rests on an unchallenged assumption that to be informal is to be spontaneous. Informal, however, more often than not refers to extempore prayer. Extempore prayer may be praying "in our own words"—i.e., without set text, script, or missal—but this is not spontaneous prayer. To extemporize prayer is often to dip into a compendium of well-worn religious clichés strung together with as much familiarity and repetition as monks reciting the Office together, or a sisterhood of nuns telling the rosary. Extempore prayers can be personal and profound but they can also be hackneyed and shallow. Because God is a good God, we are absolutely not saying that he does not hear these prayers, but we are arguing that tossing out thoughts to the heavens *can* betray a certain laziness of mind and an absence of spiritual discipline. In any case, such practices are not the same as spontaneous prayer. There will always be room for spontaneous prayer in spiritual life, for when we are truly joyful we cannot withhold our praise. And in hard times desperate words from the depths of our being are so heartfelt that they well up and brim over as naturally as tears. And yet, sometimes we find that things have come to such a pass, or that we are so low, that we have nothing spontaneous left to offer. At such a time we should welcome the prayers of the saints, for they have put into words better than we can ourselves the inarticulate feelings of our spiritual longing for God.

But in the end, whether the prayer is formal or informal, written or extempore, it is its capacity to engage us—body, mind, and soul—with God that counts.

Ortho-Doxia *Is a Holistic Response to God*

Holistic worship should enable us to engage God as the *embodied* creatures that we are. As such it should be multi-sensory, appealing not merely to the ears—through songs and sermons—but to the eyes, to touch, to taste, to smell. Sarah Coakley has suggested that Christian liturgical practices are a "socially mediated, bodily enacted, sensually attuned" means of knowing Christ.

> [W]hat *sort* of epistemological apparatus is involved in this process of liturgical response and growth in intimacy with Christ? Clearly the traditional mental faculties (intellect, will, memory) are actively involved in liturgical performance, and the intellect's significance in relation to propositional theological truth is self-evident.

> But what of the distinctly sensual dimensions of liturgy—do these not play some vital part in the growth in responsiveness to Christ's relational presence in intimacy, such as we have discussed? And do they not in some sense in turn inform our intellectual and affective responses?[5]

Coakley argues that the physical senses of sight, sound, touch, taste, and smell are related to the spiritual senses such that material sensation can, if appropriately shaped over time, increasingly mediate spiritual perception. Gregory of Nyssa, in *On the Soul and the Resurrection*, "actually makes explicit the possibility of *training* the gross physical senses so that they may come to anticipate something of the capacities of the resurrection body, and so not only sense Christ himself, but actually sense *as* he senses: 'by the very operation of our senses,' says Macrina, Gregory's sister and mentor in the dialogue, 'we are led to conceive of that reality and intelligence which surpasses the senses.'"[6] In other words, one perceives God, the truth of God, not merely through the cognitive content of the words of the liturgy and sermon but also through the sight of the stained glass windows, the carved stonework, the candles, the colorful banners, the icons, the ritual movements of the clergy around the sacred space of the building, through the smell of the incense, through the sounds of the music and bells and divine words, through the touch and taste of the bread and wine. "[A]s John Chrysostom put it in the patristic era, it is all a matter of making 'the unseen visible from the seen,' a matter of training the bodily senses in attunement with Christ's presence. In the wonderful words of Cyril of Jerusalem on the physical reception of the eucharist, 'Do not have your wrists extended or your fingers spread, but making your left hand a throne for the right, for it is about to receive a King, and cupping your palm, receive the body of Christ.'"[7]

Ortho-Doxia *Accompanies* Ortho-Praxia

Old Testament prophets were not averse to offering blistering critiques of the official cult in the name of Yhwh.[8] The point was not that there was

5. Coakley, "Beyond Belief?" (2013), 141.

6. Ibid., 143.

7. Ibid., 144.

8. See Amos 4:4–5; 5:21–27; Hos 2:13–15; 6:4–6; 8:13; 13:2; Isa 1:10–17; 29:13; 43:24; 58:6; 66:3; Mic 3:4; 6:6–8; Jer 6:19–20; 7:8–10, 17–18, 21–23; 14:12; Mal 1:10; 2:13.

a problem with cult *per se—Yhwh himself* had instituted it so he would hardly condemn it. The problem arose when priests and people offered the prescribed sacrifices and said the set prayers and yet at the same time lived lives inconsistent with the goodness of the God they professed. Sometimes they would be worshiping Yhwh *and idols*, hedging their bets. God did not accept such worship. Other times they would give praise to God with their lips but act in ways incompatible with holiness, treating other people like dirt. God said that he hated and rejected such shallow "worship."

Consider these searing words from Amos:

> I hate, I despise your feasts,
> and I take no delight in your solemn assemblies.
> Even though you offer me your burnt offerings and grain offerings,
> I will not accept them;
> and the peace offerings of your fattened animals,
> I will not look upon them.
> Take away from me the noise of your songs;
> to the melody of your harps I will not listen.
> But let justice roll down like waters,
> and righteousness like an ever-flowing stream. (Amos 5:21–24)

This is a very challenging strand in the biblical literature. And it applies to Christian worship too. Do we imagine that God will accept our worship if we are blatantly living in ways that run counter to the gospel? The answer must surely be "no," but we need to be careful not to be the first to cast stones for all the historic traditions have been counterfeit churches at times—having the form of orthodoxy but in reality serving the master of a different kingdom. In the 1930s, for example, Lutheran bishops declared that Jesus was not a Jew (and by taking away his cultural particularity they *ipso facto* denied his humanity). This distancing of Jesus from Judaism was arguably the extension of Luther's own anti-Semitism (which, lamentably, had its roots in the wider Christian tradition), and it made it easier for many German Lutherans to turn a blind eye to the Nazis' treatment of the Jews. And in this regard the Catholic Church in Nazi Germany was no better.

The Balkans provide a more contemporary example. The Orthodox Church in Serbia could rightly claim they were more sinned against than sinning if they look back to World War II when the mainly Catholic Croatians killed half a million Serbs. Under Tito, however, Yugoslavia became so secularized that by the 1990s only 10 percent of Serbs were baptized

Christians. This did not stop some of the leaders of the Orthodox Church supporting the "ethnic cleansing" of Croatians and Arabs in Bosnia. Russia cannot be exonerated over this issue either. Since the wall came down in Berlin the "churches" have been subject to the Greater Serbia program in which Serbs see themselves as racially superior to other races. Not only does this racial sense of identity lend itself to genocide but this now largely secular movement has its origins from within the Russian Orthodox Church. The second wave (1870s) of Slavophile nationalism, unlike the first wave (1840s), was anti-Semitic and deeply xenophobic.[9]

All such *anti*-gospel behavior makes the worship of those who engaged in it, while formally orthodox, utterly *un*orthodox, nay *hetero*dox.

But the godly response to such perversion is modeled by the prophets too; it is a posture of anguished commitment. Thus Jeremiah simultaneously denounces Israel's iniquity for what it is and yet remains committed to the covenant between God and the people, even in their sin. He is furious with Judah yet does not turn his back on her but weeps over her infidelity. Jeremiah condemns and laments not because he hates Judah but because he still lover her.

Ortho-Doxia *and Community*

While it is perfectly possible and indeed normal to worship God alone, Christians have *always* met together for communal worship. This is because it is important for us that God was not simply redeeming lots of individuals but a *society* of saints (and, *contra* Margaret Thatcher, there *is* such a thing as society). The church is not like a jar of sweets—a collection of individual units that can exist just as well alone as in a jar with others. In Scripture the church is a family (brothers and sisters, siblings with Christ and children of the Father), a body (1 Cor 12; Rom 12), and a temple (1 Cor 3:16–17; Eph 2:21–22). In all these images the parts are nothing without the whole, only finding their own identity in relation with others. So it is that Christian tradition has always made *communal* worship the paradigm case.

9. Walker "The Prophetic Role of Orthodoxy" (1996), 232–33.

Right Worship and Mass Media?

Does the modern world offer exciting new opportunities for worship? Many twentieth-century Christians rejoiced at the opportunities presented by the massive audiences that could be reached through television and radio. And services of worship broadcast on such media are a familiar, albeit small, part of the landscape now, so much so that we rarely stop to think about it. However, while there is some merit in such programs, especially for those who are housebound for one reason or another, Christians ought to feel somewhat uncomfortable about them. Radio and television are not neutral media but are embedded in certain forms of life. They are not interactive but inculcate passive modes of engagement. So typically those who listen to church services on the radio or watch them on television are not actively engaged in worshiping with the congregation but are passively letting it wash over them. After all, *that is how you engage radio and television.* So these media are ill suited to worship and are in danger of warping it—listeners and viewers are implicitly invited to consume the worship as a form of entertainment. The passive listening/viewing mode of radio and television are good for certain things but worship is not one of those things.

Matters are potentially somewhat different with the new phenomenon of online worship. In spite of some of the concerns raised about internet worship services, some of which we share, they are potentially *far* superior to radio and television worship. There are multiple different levels of interactive engagement involved. These online worship sites include prayer forums where people can post prayers or solicit prayer requests for specific situations, various liturgical prayer resources for personal devotion, forums in which people can chat about issues of life, faith, theology, or anything they want, blogs where people can interact with the reflections of chosen bloggers, and bookshops where you can purchase recommended books. Some sites even host online social events each week for those in the virtual community. Most importantly, for this chapter, there are live, interactive services, sometimes led by ordained clergy, in (virtual) chapels at regular set times. We shall return to this in a moment.

These online communities are usually open to anyone and everyone to drop in and out of as they see fit. However, often at their heart is a core community, those who share the vision of internet church and who have committed to its long-term good. The core-community will have special privileges and dedicated spaces for interaction. This two-level model of community allows online churches to be welcoming and inclusive while at the same time encouraging long-term committed engagement in the community. It also allows stability in the core ecclesial and theological visions of the churches.

Regarding the online worship services, these can be God-focused, gospel-shaped, Trinitarian, and unlike radio and television services they are more likely to be interactive and existentially engaged. Indeed, they can also be genuinely communal, at least to a certain extent. And they have various potential benefits. They can be a good, non-threatening first port of call for people unfamiliar with church: precisely because anonymity and opting out are far easier people may risk exploring the faith in a context like that before taking the plunge with solid people. And for Christians it can be a safe place to explore their questions about the faith. On top of that, it is a "space" that Christians from across the globe can meet to fellowship, enriching each other in the encounter.

But there are weaknesses about online church that are inherent to the medium. There is a problem with a tendency toward disembodiment of the virtual world. Christianity, in its more sane moments, has a very strong valuation of materiality, spatiality, and temporality. Christian worship has traditionally been fully embodied and multi-sensory. We eat and drink together, we share the peace by embracing, we sing together, we plunge people into water, we light candles, we lay hands on people, and so on. Online church can only approximate some of this with various degrees of verisimilitude and cannot capture the full-embodied experience. Can you baptize someone online? And even though you can share the Eucharist something is lost when it is done. Our communion with each other is represented by our sharing the *same* cup and the *same* loaf and that is simply impossible online. Instead worshipers all bring our own bread and wine to have it blessed. On top of that, it is difficult, though not impossible, to develop deep levels of community with people that you never meet face-to-face. There are some things that can only be communicated through a touch, or an embrace. Sometimes we need someone with us to help us and that too is impossible if they are locked away on the other side of a screen. And, we may ask, how easy is it to make disciples online with people we never meet in the flesh? Superficial commitment is all too easy. Thus, while we think that there are merits in churches creating forums for online worship and community these should not present themselves as *substitutes* for embodied churches but as gateways into and supplements for them.

In conclusion, we have explored in this chapter how orthodox Christian worship aspires to be God-focused, gospel-shaped, Trinitarian, existentially engaged, holistic, accompanied by right living, and practiced in community. The next chapter will develop further the connection between right worship, right belief, and *right practice*.

7

Deep Living

Orthopraxia *as Right Practice*

WE HAVE INSISTED THAT Christian faith is an existential commitment to
God in Christ and as such it involves right belief, right devotion, and right
living. In this chapter we will argue that right living is intimately entangled
with belief in God as creator and with the story of God in Christ.

Orthopraxia, right practice, is a wide-ranging concept covering everything from the ritual use of the body in worship to appropriate Christian
moral behavior. As we have already discussed public worship we shall focus
our attention here on *orthopraxia* as embodied ethical living.

The Modern World and Its Ethical Discontents

According to philosopher Alasdair MacIntyre modernity has brought
about an unnoticed ethical catastrophe in the West. The classical language
of morality remains in fragments but it has become detached from the
original theoretical context in which it made sense and has been relocated
in new contexts, acquiring new meanings in the process. So people continue to use moral language and *think* that they are engaging in the same
ethical conversation as thinkers from ancient Greece onwards, but, argues
MacIntyre, they are not. What they are really doing is a pale imitation, a
kind of pseudo-ethical discourse, because although they have retained the
vocabulary they have changed its meaning.

According to MacIntyre ethics before modernity had a threefold structure

> in which human-nature-as-it-happens-to-be (human nature in its untutored state) is initially discrepant and discordant with the precepts of ethics and needs to be transformed by the instruction of practical reason and experience into human-nature-as-it-could-be-if-it-realized-its-*telos*. . . . To say what someone *ought* to do is at one and the same time to say what course of action will in these circumstances as a matter of fact lead toward a man's true end and to say what the law, ordained by God and comprehended by reason, enjoins.[1]

We could represent this as follows:

A. human-nature-as-it-is-now

    C. ethics (the route from A to B)

B. human-nature-as-it-could-be-if-it-realized-its-telos

So ethical injunctions were situated within a scheme in which their purpose was to lead people from A *to* B. Consider the word "good" in the phrase "that is a good watch." A watch has a purpose—to tell the time accurately— and it is a good watch if it fulfills that purpose. The very "concept of a watch cannot be defined independently of the concept of a good watch."[2] Classical ethical language functioned in the same way. Humanity was understood as having an essential nature and purpose fleshed out in multiple social roles—member of family, citizen, soldier, doctor, servant of God, and so on. Thus, "'man' stands to 'good man' as 'watch' stands to 'good watch.'"[3] Whether someone or some action was "good" was determined by whether it enabled human flourishing in its designated area of human life. Thus to call something "good" was to make a *factual* assertion. Moral judgments were either factually *true* or *false*, depending on whether they did or did not lead to human flourishing.

The fundamental problem with modern ethics arose because Western thinkers since the Enlightenment have rejected B (the idea that human

---

1. MacIntyre, *After Virtue* (1985), 53; italics added.
2. Ibid., 58.
3. Ibid.

nature has a *telos*, a true goal or purpose) and retained only A and C. Thus modern ethics is based on the following scheme:

A. human-nature-as-it-is-now
C. ethics

However, ethics (C) had always been conceived in terms of its relationship to a human *telos* (B). So what is ethics all about once purpose/*telos* is removed from the picture? Modernity has created a world of facts (A) and values (C) with a great chasm between them that has proved impossible to bridge. You are left with an empirical world of facts that is devoid of values and a set of values that have proved notoriously difficult to handle. On the new view you cannot derive an "ought" (a moral imperative) from an "is" (a fact about the world) or a moral value from a fact. To better understand the problem, imagine trying to speak about a good watch if all we have are watches but no belief that they are *for* anything or have a *purpose*. In that case how should language about *good* and *bad* watches function and how can it be grounded? The same dilemma arises in ethics—once *telos* is removed ethics needs either to be abandoned or to find a new rationale.

The project of modern ethical theory, says MacIntyre, has been the story of the failed search for such a rationale. Enlightenment philosophers agreed that ethics needed founding on either the passions or on reason. David Hume tried to build upon human physiological nature. In his view, moral judgments, which move us to action, cannot be founded on reason and so must be seen as expressions of feeling. We do appeal to moral rules but these are simply useful guides to help us achieve the goals of our passions. Kant, on the other hand, argued that morality cannot be grounded on the passions and must be founded on reason. Rationality is the same for all rational creatures and so moral rules based on rationality must be universal, categorical, and internally consistent. Thus the simple maxim to test the morality of any imperative is to ask whether a rational being would will all others to always follow the rule. But both foundations have proved to be unpersuasive, leaving ethics floundering. In the nineteenth century the Utilitarianism of Bentham and Mill was an attempt to reintroduce some notion of teleology, with actions ethically vindicated (or not) by their consequences. The right actions were the actions that maximized pleasure over pain for the greatest number of people. Of course, Utilitarianism was riddled with problems (for instance, how do you quantify and compare all the many vastly different kinds of pleasures and pains?) and it too failed to be generally persuasive.

From this inevitable failure to rescue ethics from the crippling wound inflicted by the loss of human *telos*—and the consequent sundering of fact and value—flows the modern moral culture, which MacIntye describes as "emotivism." By emotivism he means the theory that moral language cannot be rationally grounded (because reason cannot help us to decide which moral principles are right) so in the end the choice of which moral principles to live by simply boils down to *personal preference*. The natural world becomes evacuated of moral values and ethics becomes relegated to the inner world of human feelings and choices. We may dress up our chosen principles in rational rhetoric (like Kantian or Utilitarian ethics) but this merely masks their true nature as no more than individual preference. Moral judgments, in the end, are neither right nor wrong, true nor false, but are simply expressions of feeling. But the insidious side to this is that "evaluative utterances can in the end have no point or use but the expression of my own feelings or attitudes and the transformation of the feelings and attitudes of others. . . . [Thus] the sole reality of distinctively moral discourse is the attempt of one will to align the attitudes, feelings, preference, and choices of another with its own. Others are always means, never end."[4] This mode of ethics boils down to attempts to manipulate others to see things my way.

In terms of Western popular culture one can see that the failure to find ethical truth through reason would lead people to think that maybe we cannot agree on right and wrong because *there is no right and wrong*, or, if there is, it is simply culture-relative or person-relative. This loss of faith in objective moral values, in turn, leads to a growing pluralism in ethical values, especially as traditional Christian values fade over time in the moral imaginations of Westerners. And, while it is not inevitable, it is hardly surprising that moral pluralism, in turn, increases the plausibility of moral relativism.

Yet this widely shared moral relativism is inconsistent. Few people seem willing to say that Hitler's extermination of six million Jews was not objectively wrong. The problem for postmodern people, of course, is that if ethics do not transcend individual opinions then *on what basis* can we say that Hitler's actions were *really* evil? Instinctively we feel that something is

4. Ibid., 24.

objectively bad but we have removed the grounds on which we can make such a claim intelligible. That is our modern moral plight.

One solution in the modern world has been the phenomenal success of the language and theory of human rights. Ironically, as Brad Gregory points out, the ethic of human rights was built upon a Christian ethical tradition that emerged first in the twelfth century. Rights were grounded in human nature, created in God's image. But with the modern need to expel God from the justification of rights the model itself is in danger of shooting itself in the foot. Such rights are certainly not "self-evident"—Thomas Jefferson could only get away with that claim because he was speaking from a culture that was dominated by Christian thought—so on what grounds can we make claims for universal human rights? If naturalism is correct then such rights *cannot* be more than human constructions, useful fictions that are created rather than discovered. Indeed, all secular attempts to provide such grounds have failed and the theory of rights—a centerpiece of the secular society—is left hanging in the air, as if by sheer will power. It is somewhat reminiscent of Wile E. Coyote who, in pursuit of the Road Runner, runs off the edge of a cliff without realizing it; he continues to run for some time until it dawns on him that there is nothing holding him up and he suddenly drops. Without foundations rights theory, ubiquitous as it is, seems increasingly to boil down to a simple exercise of power—different interest groups simply *asserting* that they have a right to this or that in the hope of getting what they want.

The modern state has committed itself to use its power to defend the rights of individuals to choose to do *whatever* they wish (so long as their actions do not impinge negatively on the rights of other autonomous individuals to do whatever they wish). Public ethics has been transformed and reduced to the protection of the individual's right to realize his or her own desires and choices. Anything more substantive has been relegated to the private world. "Politics subsumes ethics and power displaces reason once morality is subjectivized."[5]

Within Christendom good and bad, right and wrong, were not simply human inventions. They were determined by the transcendent realm and the very structures of the creation that God had made, by the kinds of creatures human beings were (in the image of God), the purposes for which God had made them, and the commands that God had given to guide them. Virtues were those dispositions that led toward those divinely

5. Gregory, *The Unintended Reformation* (2012), 230.

appointed ends, and vices those that led away from them. Both Catholics and Protestants agreed that right and wrong were *objective truths about the world*. But as the theological framework upon which such a moral vision depends loses its public acceptance the vision itself loses its basis. *This* is the social location in which Christians now need to act according to the gospel.

Ortho-doxy and *Ortho-Praxis* 1: Beliefs

We have already said that Christian ethics was traditionally understood in terms of a theology in which humans are God's creatures and have a set of purposes. Divine laws were not random prohibitions and prescriptions but were related to the kinds of creatures that God had created humans to be. Christian virtues such as faith, hope, and love were not arbitrarily selected but were similarly tied to God's purposes for humanity.

Here we need to introduce the critical role of narrative in traditional moral life because it was primarily narrative that carried the pre-modern ethical vision. "I can only answer the question, 'What am I to do?' if I can answer the prior question, 'Of what story or stories do I find myself a part?'"[6] This is because our stories tell us where we are from and where we are going and, thus, who we are. This is certainly the case with the biblical narratives. "Stories are the secret reservoir of values: change the stories individuals or nations tell themselves, and you change the individuals or nations."[7] They provide individuals-in-community with models of vice and virtue in the context of various different relationships; they teach us to pay attention both to general moral features in diverse situations (and to pay heed to moral rules) but also to consider carefully the particularity of each specific situation (because general rules may not apply in certain situations and wisdom is needed to discern that). Stories can also train us in the importance of emotional perception essential to ethical rationality—moral wisdom is not about a passionless application of some moral formula but is essentially emotionally engaged. Stories (both fictional and factual) thus offer training in ethical perception.

More than merely displaying virtues and in-forming ethical perception, stories can shape the very grammar of ethics, the contours of what we *mean* by goodness, greed, gratitude, and love. While it may be possible, as Martha Nussbaum proposes, to offer a generic Aristotelian ethic that

6. MacIntyre, *After Virtue* (1985), 216.
7. Okri, *Birds of Heaven* (1995), 21.

transcends different traditions,[8] it is not possible, so we maintain, to offer a *rich* and *robust* moral vision apart from the specific narratives of a moral tradition. Robert C. Roberts makes the following observations about the story of Jesus in Christian ethics:

> The narrative of the incarnation, death, and resurrection of the Son of God does not just dramatically display a set of virtues with a special grammar, but is itself taken up in the grammar of the virtues of those who accept the story and become members of the community. Compassion is seeing in the faces of the sufferers one ministers to the face of the incarnate Son who died for them; contrition is both sadness for sins committed against the God whose Son is the main character in the story and comfort that this man's death is one's own righteousness; gratitude is first of all for the act of God recounted in the story; hope is first of all for the resurrection for which the risen Jesus is the firstfruits . . . [T]he main function of the narrative in the Christian community . . . is not to display the Christian virtues, but to take its place in the grammar of those virtues.[9]

This claim can perhaps best be illustrated by the way in which Saint Paul fleshes out his community ethic of love by means of the gospel story. Michael Gorman, in his book *Cruciformity*, shows that Paul's whole approach to Christian living was controlled by the story of the crucified and risen Messiah. The master story for Paul is seen in the Christ hymn of Philippians 2:5b–11.

> . . . Christ Jesus, who, though he was in the form of God, did not count equality with God a thing to be grasped [i.e., exploited for his own advantage], but emptied himself, by taking the form of a servant, being born in the likeness of men. And being found in human form, he humbled himself by becoming obedient to the point of death, even death on a cross. Therefore God has highly exalted him and bestowed on him the name that is above every name, so that at the name of Jesus every knee should bow, in heaven and on earth and under the earth, and every tongue confess that Jesus Christ is Lord, to the glory of God the Father. (ESV)

Instead of using his equality with God to his own advantage he "emptied himself" and "humbled himself" for the sake of others. Key aspects of this narrative are (a) humiliation followed by exaltation, (b) voluntary

8. Nussbaum, "Non-Relative Virtues" (1993).
9. Roberts, "Narrative Ethics" (1999), 479

self-humbling, following the pattern: *Although [high status], not [selfishness] but [self-abasement/slavery]* (c) the pattern of obedience to God.

Now this very pattern becomes the heart of Christian ethics: "For Paul, to be in Christ is to be a living exegesis of this narrative of Christ, a new performance of the original drama of exaltation following humiliation, of humiliation as the voluntary renunciation of rights and selfish gain in order to serve and obey."[10] Gorman goes on to identify four patterns of cruciformity in Paul's letters

1. Cruciformity as *faithful obedience* (faith)

2. Cruciformity as *voluntary self-emptying* (love)

3. Cruciformity as life-giving suffering and transformative *power in weakness* (power)

4. Cruciformity as a *prelude to resurrection* and exaltation (hope)

It is the second pattern that particularly concerns us here. That love is at the core of Christian ethics is not especially controversial (Rom 13:8; Gal 5:14), but the critical gospel insight is that the *meaning* of "love" is redefined for the followers of Jesus by the master story of Christ crucified. Indeed, Paul never mentions Christ's love without referring to the story of the cross (Gal 2:19–21; Rom 8:34–35a, 37; 2 Cor 5:14–15). Love does not seek its own advantage but is characterized by the renunciation of rights and status in pursuit of the good of the other (1 Cor 8:1; 13:5). We might compare this with John's first epistle: "*This* is love: not that we loved God, but that he loved us and sent his Son as an atoning sacrifice for our sins. Dear friends, since God so loved us, we also ought to love one another" (1 John 4:10–11; NIV). He's saying that if you want to understand what love is then consider how God gave that which was most precious to him for the sake of those who did not even love him, people to whom he was in no debt. *That* is love. Now go and do likewise.

Returning to Paul, we need to notice that Paul recites the Christ hymn in Philippians 2:6–11 precisely as a story to ground the Philippians' relationships with each other; his goal is *formative* rather than simply informative: "Do nothing from selfish ambition or conceit, but in humility count others more significant than yourselves. Let each of you look not only to his own interests, but also to the interests of others. Have this mind among yourselves, which is yours in Christ Jesus, who, though he was in the form

10. Gorman, *Cruciformity* (2001), 92.

of God, did not count equality with God a thing to be grasped . . ." (Phil 2:3–6). Jesus' love is sacrificial and costly, self-giving, and status-renouncing, and such love should mark those "in Christ." Gorman demonstrates that this Philippians 2 pattern appears over and over again in Paul's ethical teachings on issues as diverse as eating kosher food, behavior at the Lord's Supper, the use of spiritual gifts, the treatment of sinners within the church, financial giving, responding to enemies, hospitality, Christian unity, the treatment of slaves, relations between husbands and wives, and the challenges of his own apostolic ministry.

The community of the baptized are those who have been joined to Christ by the Holy Spirit and who have united their own stories to the story of Jesus. The Christian journey, for Paul, is a journey toward being conformed to the image of the Messiah and what that means is *cruci*-formity. It is a story that links into a bigger story of Adam created in God's image for glory, about the defacing of the image and its recovery. It is a story that tells us where we are from, where we are, where we are going, and how God is going to get us there. It is a story that subverts all the alternative stories in both the ancient and the modern worlds, reconfiguring ethics in the process.

The subsequent Christian tradition has also sought, in various ways and with varying degrees of success, to develop patterns of living consistent with this master narrative. One thinks, for instance, of the traditional Christian practice of almsgiving, the giving of financial and material resources to the poor in fulfillment of God's mission to the poor. For the first four and a half centuries almsgiving was a significant aspect of the church's life. Now, the practice was not unique to Christians but was inherited by them from Judaism and also practiced by pagans. Yet Christians did seek to reshape it in accord with biblical teaching and the Jesus story. For instance, almsgiving among pagans was often used to further the status of the giver. Christians were often influenced by this approach too but church leaders such as John Chrysostom sought to clarify for his churches that for Christians almsgiving must not be done for personal gain. Purging the practice from selfish motives was part of the gospel leavening that Christian leaders sought to bring.

> For John [Chrysostom], the practice of almsgiving was essential to the Christian mission. Almsgiving was confessional as a material representation of the spiritual presence of Christ in the Christian mission, ceremonial in its essentiality for biblical ecclesiology, and

practical in order to maximize effectiveness for each circumstance. In the Eastern Empire of the fourth century, Christian churches and their leadership had become some of the most influential voices in culture and society. The Christian mission among the poor gave advocacy to many who had previously been ignored. Through John's leadership in Antioch, and later in Constantinople, the responsibility to care for the needy became a top priority for Christian churches. The Christian mission to the poor was a thrust which enabled the working poor to gain the possibility of social progress while the destitute attained new levels of representation. In Antioch, almsgiving in the churches was identified as the most generous activity among the poor. Christian benevolence clearly demonstrated the commitment of the Christian mission to transmit the hope of the gospel among all people regardless of ethnic, demographic, or economic distinctions.[11]

While not without problems, the early Christian approach to almsgiving is, argues Eric Costanzo in his book *Harbor for the Poor*, an important untapped resource for contemporary Christian mission to the poor.

Ortho-doxy and *Ortho-Praxis* 2: Worship

Ortho-praxis is also inextricable from right worship. As we saw in the last chapter, the extent to which worship is accompanied by failure to love is the extent to which it is a failure to offer Christian worship. We can reinforce that point from Paul's comments about the Eucharist in 1 Corinthians 11:17–34.

Here a little background on the politics of the Eucharist may help. As Alan Streett has shown,[12] the Lord's Supper was a subversive, non-violent, yet anti-imperial meal. The early Eucharist was modeled on the two-part structure of the Roman banquet with a *deipnon* (main course) and a *symposium*. The symposium focused on dessert, the consumption of alcohol, and a wide range of post-meal entertainment including music, lectures, debates, drama, games, and dancing. Banquets were events in which all free men participated and in which the ideology of the empire was reinforced. The social stratification of Rome was embodied and perpetuated (this was not a meal for women or for slaves) and libations were poured out to Caesar and the gods of Rome.

11. Costanzo, *Harbor for the Poor* (2013), 138.
12. Streett, *Subversive Meals* (2013).

The Christian meal followed the two-part pattern (meal and after-meal activities) but was suffused with a very different set of social and political norms. The values of the Lord's Supper were those of the Jewish Passover feast (a celebration of political liberation from oppression) mediated and transformed by Jesus at his Last Supper. Jesus had used meals throughout his ministry to offer a counter-imperial vision of society, which he called the kingdom of God. He used meals to include those excluded by imperialistic eating codes of stratification, patronage, and power politics. The Last Supper itself—where, against all social conventions, the Master washed the feet of his disciples—set a pattern that his disciples would continue to follow.

The Eucharist was an inclusive, community-building feast in which Roman values were resisted in numerous ways. It was not Caesar that was honored as "Lord," "Savior," and "Son of God" (all titles he claimed), but rather Jesus, *a criminal executed by Rome as an insurrectionist!* And around this table gather not merely free men but also women and, even more shockingly, slaves. All meet and eat together as equals, as one body "in the Lord." At this meal songs and psalms were sung, prayers were said, and readings given from Israel's Scripture, from Gospels, and from letters by apostles, prophets, and evangelists. All of these proclaimed a different kingdom from Rome and a different king from Caesar.

However, in Corinth it appears that the wealthier members of the congregation were using the communal meal as a place to reinforce the social divisions between themselves and the poorer members, divisions imported into the church setting from the culture around them. So in these meals the rich ate their fill while the poor went hungry. Paul is appalled. A meal intended to celebrate the unity and equality of the community, the body of Christ, has become a means for undermining those very things. Rather than the act of worship subverting the inequalities of Roman society the Roman values had corrupted it. This meal you eat, says Paul, has been poisoned by anti-gospel values and is consequently not the *Lord's* Supper, because by humiliating those who have nothing you have failed to discern, nay you have *despised*, the church as Christ's body. For this reason, he adds, divine judgment had come upon you. As Gordon Smith comments, "We should call a meal the Lord's Supper only when the only possible basis for our eating together is our common identity in Jesus and our common communion with one another and with the living Christ."[13]

13. Smith, *A Holy Meal* (2005), 54.

But we might also consider how the Eucharist was supposed to function in the community. This very ritual meal was, if practiced correctly, packed full of ethical implications. To celebrate the *Lord's* Supper is to celebrate the equality of all those in the community, irrespective of their social status in the wider world; it is to value each and every other as one loved by Christ; it is to receive on the same terms as every one else the unmerited grace of God; it is to make central the self-giving love of the Lord at the center of one's existence; it is to make one's primary allegiance to the body of Christ rather than to the demands of any nation or race.

With regard to the last we would draw attention to William Cavanaugh's examination of the response of the Catholic Church in Chile to the torture program of General Pinochet. At first the Church was in the grip of a bad theology that saw itself as responsible for spiritual lives but considered the state as ruling over the bodies of the people. The power of the state over the bodies of its citizens is demonstrated in its power, in certain circumstances, to imprison bodies, to demand that they go to war, and to execute them. Torture is the supreme demonstration of a state's power over bodies. But once the Church got a better grip on what the Eucharist was about it began to refuse to hand over the bodies of its members to the state. The Chilean state has been secretly "disappearing" people in order to make public confrontation more difficult (they could always deny that anything has happened) so the Church had to develop strategies to make the invisible tortured bodies visible. The state wanted victims not martyrs, which is why it used secrecy. So the Church claimed the victims as Christian martyrs. Thus the state's abduction and torture of individuals was no longer a matter of individuals, a *private* matter, but an attack *on the Church*. What the state does to individuals it does to the community. It was the Eucharist—focused as it is on Jesus' tortured body—that provided the worshipful focus for the claiming of the victims as part of the community. This move allowed there to be mobilization against the torture program of the state. The Church organized very visible practical help for victims (legal, medical, food provision, job training, etc.), which served to knit the body of Christ together in eucharistic ways. The Church also organized subversive street liturgies to make the tortured body of Christ visible in ways that brought the unwanted attention that the government sought to avoid. And the Church very publically excommunicated—and thus denied Holy Communion to—anyone involved in torture. In this way the Church showed that the body of Christ was associated with the tortured not the torturers. To torture is to act in ways incompatible with what Eucharist is about.

> Unity in the church is much more than agreement on doctrine or the general ability of the members of the church to get along, nor is it just participation in a common project or community. It is participation in Christ, and so requires a narrative display of the life, death, and resurrection of Jesus Christ. Unity is based on assimilation to Christ, and so the unity and the identity of the church are the same issue. Jesus was tortured to death. Tortured and torturers in the same church therefore threaten the transparency of the church as the body of Christ.[14]

So we see that rightly aligned worship can fund rightly aligned practice in radical ways.

Holy Living in Modernity and Postmodernity

Living godly lives has always been a challenge—from Paul's day to our own. Christendom presented a whole new set of challenges as Christianity gradually became the cultural norm and many of those in churches were less than fully committed. In Christendom Christians often lived very questionable lives. There was little self-deception about this because the church has a clear awareness—articulated most astutely by Augustine in his distinction between "the city of God" and "the city of men"—of the gap between ideal and reality. Of course, the ideal was still to be pursued, thus arose many renewal movements that sought to close the gap. Nevertheless, there was general agreement on what a good life looked like. Modernity and postmodernity have changed that. The loss of the understanding of human life having a *telos* has thrown the project of ethics into crisis. And the loss of the specifically Christian story as a framework for the good life has sawn off the branch that Western moral life has perched on for centuries. It has taken several generations for the implications of that loss to work through in practice, indeed it remains the case that Western ethics are still parasitic on Christianity to a far greater extent than many like to admit, but things are changing.

The danger for Christians is what it has always been: that like the wealthy Corinthians we can easily draw our ethical values and imperatives from the culture at large rather than from the gospel. Social pressure of

14. Cavanaugh, *Torture and Eucharist* (1998), 247.

various degrees and in various modes is inevitably put on churches to fit in with cultural norms. When Christian values clash with those norms there are tensions. Inevitably individual Christians within congregations are fed the same diet of values—through novels, television, films, and the like—as the rest of society. And you are what you eat so inevitably such values shape Christian believers, just as they shape others. Certain values start to appear to be plain "common sense." One can quite easily find churches embracing a moral vision that is not in-formed by the gospel. Often secular values are dressed up in a superficial Christian costume to give it some credibility. And this is not simply a problem for liberal Christians; it is just as common among conservatives.

Consider this example from the liberal end of the church: more than a few liberal Christians take it as obvious that a pregnant woman has a straightforward right to choose whether or not to carry her child to term. Freedom to choose is *the* most fundamental value in modern Western cultures and so the right to autonomy over our own bodies is highly prized. This is often (though not inevitably) taken to mean that valuing women as human beings, as agents with control over their own bodies, requires accepting their legal and moral right to have an abortion if they so choose. Liberal Christians with pro-choice sympathies embrace this modern Western view. They further argue that the Bible does not address the issue of abortion so there is no "biblical" view on the subject. Christians are thus free to be pro-choice.

However, before rushing to such a position we should note that the early church inhabited a culture in which abortion and infanticide were common and yet it chose to swim against the cultural flow and oppose such practices.[15] The rationale was simply that killing a fetus was killing a human being and, hence, inconsistent with the Bible's teaching on not taking human life. This stance has been the consistent witness of the church until modern times (and remains the majority view). That should at very least give us pause for thought. Although the Bible does not directly address the matter of abortion the church has always interpreted biblical teaching

15. Witnesses from the first and second centuries are the *Didache* 2.2; the *Epistle of Barnabas* 19; the *Apocalypse of Peter* 25; Tertullian, *De anima* 37; and Athenagoras, *Plea for Christians* 35. Later writers, such as Augustine, *On Marriage and Concupiscence* 17; Jerome, *Letter to Eustochium*; and Basil of Caesarea, *First Canonical Epistle*, concur. Cyprian even described it as heresy (*Letter 48*). It was, furthermore, condemned by three local church councils—the council of Elvira (fourth century), the council of Ancyra (fourth century), and the council of Trullo (sixth century).

(e.g., on unborn life and on the need to protect human life) to entail that abortion is usually wrong.

We are not seeking to argue that every instance of abortion is wrong—each case must be considered in its particularity and there may well be exceptional circumstances—but it does seem that at very least the tradition should incline the church to have *a presumption against abortion*. Abortion is not merely some morally neutral "choice" such as which career path to follow or whether or not to marry. The church must not simply rubber-stamp the morality of the culture around it. Rather, we must always ask ourselves the question: Is the choice in question consistent with the gospel story? At the same time, if the church is to maintain its historic stance it needs to apply exactly the same question to itself concerning the way it treats women facing the decision of abortion. What kind of behavior does the gospel story demand? It must involve self-sacrificial love, practical care, and ongoing support for women in what are often very difficult circumstances. And a gospel-shaped church must also offer unconditional love and support to those women who choose to have abortions.

But it is not just liberals: American evangelicals are often uncritically supportive of free-market global capitalism; of the quick resort to military firepower to solve complex problems; of whatever policies the State of Israel chooses to employ in the West Bank and Gaza; of shunning the concerns of environmentalists in the name of the freedom of individuals and corporations to make money; of the priority of the nuclear family; of the right of citizens to amass lethal weapons as they see fit; of the centrality of the individual; of the right to be super wealthy (indeed, for some this is proof of God's blessing); of resisting attempts by the government to provide for the poorest citizens. All this is simply "common sense Christianity" to more than a few American evangelicals. And one does not have to go too far back in American history to find many evangelicals supporting slavery as a Christian institution (although this issue was always very divisive). Now all of these are complex issues and we are not suggesting that the real gospel-shaped response is to be an anti-capitalist pacifist committed to big government and tree hugging. The issues are not black and white and require careful reflection and nuanced responses. But we suggest that many of these common evangelical attitudes need to come under the same gospel scrutiny and judgment that liberalism does. They arguably owe as much or more to worldly culture than to Scripture, tradition, or the evangel.

The call of the gospel is not toward liberalism or conservativism—it is toward radicalism. That is to say, it is a call *back to the root*, to the gospel story itself. Such a journey will at times look quite liberal and at other times very conservative but that is neither here nor there. The fundamental and uncomfortable question we need to revisit again and again is this: What ethic is embodied in the gospel as set forth in Scripture, and encapsulated in the creeds and the worship practices of the church?

The call to deep church is a call to an ongoing discernment of the gospel-shaped response to the complex world in which we live. Our prayer, to adapt a line from Naomi Shemer's poem "Jerusalem of God," should ever be, "For all your songs, Lord, may we be a violin."

8

Deep Transformation

Recovering Catechesis

"Do not let the world squeeze you into its mold"

THE GOSPEL IS ABOUT communal and individual transformation: a community—the church—being conformed to the image of Jesus, becoming more human. But Paul warns the Christians in Rome not to be "conformed to this world" (Rom 12:2) or, in the words of J. B. Phillips, not to let the world "squeeze you into its mold." Yet the world is constantly shaping us with its values, beliefs, priorities, and practices. All day every day we are exposed to a constant flow of formative inputs and often we are oblivious to it for it is the very air we breathe. In chapter 2 we saw the way in which Christian faith and practice can be impacted by a myriad of social factors. Consider the influences forming an ordinary devout Christian. We have spent many hours exposed to the implicit worldview of our secular education at school and university, we hang out with friends with very different beliefs and lifestyles, we listen to music with lyrics that reflect certain ideas and values sung by pop celebrities whose very public lives embody a dream quite different from that of a gospel-shaped life. Every day we watch movies and TV shows and read books and magazines that present models for life that tell us "the way things are." We spend more and more time online—on our computers and mobile phones—with instant access to information and images and people in ways unimaginable a generation ago. We are exposed to an *astronomical* amount of advertising pitched with the deliberate aim of shaping our lifestyle ambitions in ways that bear little resemblance to Christian ambitions. Whether we want it or not we are subjected to a constant torrent of life-shaping influences. And it is not simply the explicit *content* of, for instance, mass media entertainment that shapes us. The very contours of modern life in the West embody a whole set of values and beliefs that we simply take on board without noticing. They are so much part of the furniture of our environment that we don't even see them. Consider mass media entertainment (TV, cinema, music, magazines, iPods, YouTube, facebook, twitter, game consoles, etc.). In his insightful book *iPod, YouTube, Wii Play* Brent Laytham argues that entertainment has become a multitrillion dollar cultural superpower with structures and processes aimed to "direct our attention, foster desire, generate symbols, structure activity, orient goals, shape relationships, and form community."[1] He speaks of how the industry aims to affect our

- *Heart:* by fostering desires for its various products.

- *Head and shoulders, knees and toes:* by soliciting our desire to play (in order for it to make profit).

- *Eyes and ears:* by constantly seeking to distract us and capture our attention.

- *Calendars and clocks:* by reshaping our patterns of work and play, indoctrinating us with the idea that free-time is me-time, then seeking to take over our "leisure time," colonizing our evenings, scheduling our weekends, ordering our years with seasons, championships, festivals, finales, and pilgrimages. Our whole experience of and relationship with time is thus reordered.

- *Family, friends, and fans:* the broadcast media—radio, then television, then the internet—has changed the patterns of association for entertainment (*who* we "associate" with and *how* we associate with them). By reaching larger and larger audiences those audiences move from embodied live events into homes and then into the bedrooms of individuals reconfiguring who audiences are and how they interact. Something of this is provocatively captured in the title of Sherry Turkle's book on the impact of technology on social relationships, *Alone Together: Why We Expect More from Technology and Less from Each Other.*

---

1. Laytham, *iPod, YouTube, Wii Play* (2012), 3.

Such astonishing formative power is not something Christians can be indifferent about because we too are concerned with making disciples. Laytham argues that we need to navigate a course between the Scylla of media idolatry and the Charybdis of technophobia. To this end he suggests that we consider the entertainment industry—which is more than the sum of its parts—to be a principality and power that seeks to "captivate our gaze, colonize our imaginations, and capture our allegiance."[2] It is a good part of creation that is there to serve real, though limited, goods but it has overstretched its bounds and seeks to elevate itself—offering its limited goods as absolute necessities—and to invite us to bow down and worship it by offering it more and more time and money. Laytham's basic route of resistance is to put mass media entertainment in its place by welcoming it as a *trivial* pursuit—something positive and good yet of limited value—and refusing its pretensions to ultimacy.

The way in which modern Westerners have been sculpted into consumers has had implications for Christian discipleship, for worship, for spirituality. The church needs to be a different kind of community but that will not happen without intentionality because we are talking about swimming against a very powerful flow. That cannot be done without insight and effort.

As we saw in chapter 2, living as a Christian in modernity and postmodernity is quite different from living as a Christian before the Reformation. The sacred canopy of a Christian culture is now virtually gone and the social structures that made Christian belief and lifestyle plausible are no longer in place. It is harder to believe than it used to be—not because there are better arguments against Christianity that there used to be but simply because the plausibility structures are not in place.

If we want to be conformed to the image of Christ, if we are serious about spiritual formation and discipleship and the plausibility of Christianity in the modern West, then going to a church meeting for a couple of hours a week and having a five-minute "quiet time" each day is hardly going to do the trick. It is like putting out a house fire with a handkerchief. The churches need to get serious about rebuilding plausibility structures, about spiritual formation, and about theological education if we are to stand any chance of shaping a healthy church in the twenty-first century.

In ancient Greece *paideia* referred to the education of model citizens for the city. It referred not so much "to the principles and practice of

2. Ibid., 21.

teaching as the formative task of transmitting a cultural heritage in order to school virtue and cultivate character."[3] In this chapter we are arguing that churches need to be preoccupied with kingdom *paideia* and that this starts with catechesis. Catechesis, in turn, should be the prolegomenon to a life-long educational process in and for a deep church.

Learning from the Early Church

Yet again the early church may prove to be a resource for remembering our future. In postchristendom the church finds itself in a situation that has some analogies with that of the church before Constantine's conversion. The early *ekklesia* also was a minority community, often a despised minority, whose faith was not reinforced in the world around them. If they went out of their houses they would find the pagan worldview of Rome manifested in the ubiquitous temples and shrines, the politics, the art, the commerce, the public entertainments, and the ethical practices. It is safe to say that the plausibility structures of the Roman Empire were not ones that functioned to reinforce Christian faith! Quite the contrary, the Empire worked hard to project a world for its citizens in which the glory of Rome and of Caesar dazzled through the buildings and statues and festivals and legends and public entertainments. To proclaim Jesus, rather than Caesar, as Lord and Savior was to swim against the flow. That took a renewed imagination that could see the world through different eyes. And *that* took catechesis, education into the faith.

The early church took catechesis *very* seriously. According to the third-century *Apostolic Tradition*, catechesis was a journey that lasted for three years. The Synod of Elvira in the fourth century even made provisions for a five-year catechesis. This was no six-week Introduction to Christianity course! They knew that pagan people entering the community were not coming in as blank slates ready to be written on by the Spirit but were coming in already covered in scribbles—long-term exposure to practices and beliefs that the church considered demonic. Such converts were coming already pre-formed, or de-formed, from years of exposure to influences that ran counter to the subversive gospel of God. So the church, especially after it moved into primarily pagan rather than Jewish contexts, did not simply let people straight into the community. Instead, catechesis functioned as a kind of decompression chamber that took those seeking entry into the

3. Walker and Wright, "A Christian University Imagined" (2004), 58.

church on a transformative journey, climaxing in baptism and full entry into the Christian community.

One of the downsides of Christendom was that as the culture became more Christianized the demands of catechesis became a lot less rigorous because it was expected that people would learn to be Christian through the culture. And to some extent they did. However, the withering of catechetical formation led to a growth of Christians with confused understanding of Christian faith and ambiguous practice of it. But the new cultural context in which the Western church finds itself creates an opportunity to rediscover catechesis.

Dimensions of Catechesis

Catechesis Is Learning to Worship

Christianity is not beliefs about God plus behavior. . . . To become a disciple is not a matter of a new or changed self-understanding, but rather to become part of a different community with a different set of practices.

For example, I am sometimes confronted by people who are not Christians but who say they want to know about Christianity. . . . After many years of vain attempts to "explain" God as Trinity, I now say, "Well, to begin with we Christians have been taught to pray, 'Our Father, who art in heaven . . .'" I then suggest that a good place to begin to understand what we Christians are about is to join me in that prayer.

For to learn to pray is no easy matter but requires much training, not unlike learning to lay bricks. It does no one any good to believe in God, at least the God we find in Jesus of Nazareth, if they have not learned to pray. To learn to pray means that we must acquire humility not as something we try to do, but as commensurate with the practice of prayer. In short, we do not believe in God, become humble, and *then* learn to pray, but in learning to pray we humbly discover we cannot do other than believe in God.

But, of course, to learn to pray requires we learn to pray with other Christians. It means we must learn the disciplines necessary to worship God. Worship, at least for Christians, is the activity in which all our skills are ordered. That is why there can be no separation of Christian morality from Christian worship.

As Christians, *our worship is our morality for it is in worship we find ourselves engrafted into the story of God.* It is in worship that we acquire the skills to acknowledge who we are—sinners.[4]

Praise, thanksgiving, adoration, confession, and intercession do not come easily. What should we say? How should we say it? When? For how long?—Lord, teach us how to pray. Worship is a learned set of practices, and they are formative practices. So a *fundamental* part of catechesis must be to teach people to engage in worship. Such learning cannot simply be didactic—teaching *about* good worship—but must also be a regular, engaged participation in communal worship.

But ortho-dox Christians will want to learn to give God "right glory" and will thus be concerned to teach people to worship *well*. This protracted spiritual formation must involve a rounded approach to worship that inducts people into a wide range of important postures in the presence of God; not merely praise and adoration—which make up almost the entirety of much charismatic worship—but also penitence, confession, lament, supplication, thanksgiving, silent contemplation, and attentive listening. People also need to learn to pray with and for others, and they need to learn how to receive prayer.

Worshiping well also means learning the appropriate vocabulary for prayer. This is imbibed through simply being part of a worshiping community over time. One helpful practice is learning to pray the prayers of the church—whether we are in a cathedral, a chapel, or at home. This is a practice rejected by many committed Christians because it seems to them to be "second-hand prayer" (= second best, discarded, outdated, or inferior prayer). They eschew formal prayers because, being second-hand, they are not "our" prayers and consequently we have doubts about their efficacy and their authenticity. But praying the prayers of the church is to pray not with second-class material despoiled by time, but handed-on treasures that resist and overcome the corrosions of time. In short, we read the texts of our spiritual exemplars, so why not pray the prayers of the saints and make them our own?

Those who do not feel comfortable with a formal liturgy may find, on examination, that they are closer to set texts than they realize. For example, we all pray the Lord's Prayer because it comes straight from the lips of Jesus. But we probably also pray the prayers of David because they come straight from his heart to our own. When we pray using his words, "a broken and

4. Hauerwas, "How We Lay Bricks" (2010), 51.

contrite heart, O God, you will not despise" (Ps 51:17), we do it with deep-felt conviction and remorse, not with a sense of parroting somebody else's sentiments. We teach the faith of the church, we preach the gospel of Jesus Christ, so it is natural—not artificial or contrived—that we follow Jesus in praying to the Father and, like Jesus, make the psalms of David our own. It is difficult to change habits of a lifetime and switch from individual prayers in our own words to handed-on prayers, but we may find that we have been unwittingly praying church prayers for years: to be familiar with the corpus of Charles Wesley's hymns, for example, is already to be saturated in prayerful prose and rhyme—of praise, intercession, and contemplation.

Worshiping well also involves learning how to engage *the body* in worship. Modernity encouraged a focus on the cerebral side of worship—getting the words right in the sermons and prayers. But humans are embodied beings and need to learn to respond aright to God in embodied ways. One's physical posture when worshiping does not simply communicate one's inner attitude, it also *shapes* it. If we slouch with our hands in our pockets as we confess our sins that doesn't merely express an inappropriately laid back frame of mind; it *reinforces* it. *To change the posture can re-poise the heart.* So standing, kneeling, raising hands, closing the eyes, opening the eyes, looking up, bowing the head, sharing the peace, moving forward to take the Eucharist, making the sign of the cross, dancing, clapping, laying on hands, and so on, are not merely secondary fluff.

This is about learning to worship in an engaged, holistic way. To speak of what the body does as "mere outward religion" is to underestimate the ways in which we can know and experience God through our body. Anthropologist Talal Asad astutely comments that it is not a lack of religious education that leads to the lack of faith in secular Europe but "untaught bodies."[5]

Catechesis Is Learning Basic Theology

Let us be frank: the man and woman in the pew are often woefully ignorant about their faith. Sometimes, in the very place you would expect the greatest knowledge and enthusiasm for Christian teaching and doctrinal commitment—that is, in what the Americans call the "Bible churches"—there hangs a pall of a "know-nothing" Christianity. To be sure, they often know

5. Asad, "Remarks on the Anthropology of the Body" (1997), 48; quoted in Coakley, "Beyond 'Belief'" (2013), 132.

the latest fads brought to their attention by audio- and video-taped ministries from itinerant evangelists, but they dry up when asked to articulate the great truths of the gospel. Catechesis could make a big difference here.

What a deep church needs today is *a theology of Christian basics.* A good place to start for adults would be at the center of faith with the great hymn of affirmation that "Jesus Christ is Lord" (Phil 2:11). From this catechumens can move "further in and further down" (to adapt Lewis) to a deeper understanding of the Trinity where, like St. John of the Cross, we find ourselves lost for words at the ineffable mystery of a God who is beyond our understanding, yet who has chosen to reveal himself in the person of Jesus of Nazareth (in whom all the fullness of the Godhead dwells). It is through the mediation of the revealed Lord Jesus that we have direct access to God the Father in the abiding presence of the Holy Spirit.

Educationalists for a deep church need to start as they mean to go on: after a basic introduction to the Christian faith on the person and work of Christ, the Holy Trinity, and God's love toward his creation (the "grand narrative" of faith), young Christians need to be encouraged to learn more. Having found for themselves the primary source of faith, God himself, Christian disciples will want to go on to become acquainted with the secondary sources (the saints and the theologians) who illuminate God's self-revelation like a good commentary sheds light on an ancient text.

Catechesis Is Learning to Read the Bible

The Bible is a text that to modern Westerners seems to speak from "along time ago, in a galaxy far far away . . ." And as the practice of Bible-reading is no longer passed on in the general culture of post-Christendom the Bible has come to seem increasingly alien and irrelevant. To read the Bible well one must be *taught.*

First and foremost this is learning to understand the broad sweep of the biblical story—from creation through fall and redemption to new creation, from Genesis to Revelation. It is learning to understand one's own life in relation to that story. In this way we see the Bible *as a whole*—a grand narrative—and not simply a compilation of timeless, blessed thoughts.

Second, it is learning some simple hermeneutical guidelines for rightly understanding texts in historical and literary contexts. For instance, one shouled learn a basic understanding of genre, of interpreting parts in the light of the whole, and of consulting a commentary to get some historical and literary background.

Third, it is about learning from the wisdom of traditional Christian Bible interpretative strategies—reading in the light of the rule of faith, christological reading, typological reading, even controlled versions of allegorical interpretation.

Fourth, it is about learning traditional Christian practices of devotional reading—lectio divina, praying the Psalms, Ignatian imaginative reading, and so on.

Catechesis Is about Character Formation and Learning Holy Living

Christian holiness is not an empty space, a mere absence of bad deeds created by following a rigorous set of "thou shalt not" rules. It is perfectly possible to avoid stealing, killing, adultery, gossip, even drinking and swearing, without being holy. Holiness is not an absence but a positive *presence*—it is a character defined by God's love; it is a pattern of life shaped by the cruciform narrative of God in Christ. Holiness is not dry and stuffy but beautiful. Conforming our lives to the pattern of Christ is a work of the Holy Spirit but it is a divine work that we are called to co-operate with, in community. It is a long journey with twists and turns and ups and downs, with periods of radical transformation and long stretches where little seems to change.

Becoming more like Jesus involves the formative practices of worship, of studying Scripture prayerfully, and of intentionally developing new patterns of speaking and acting.

In worship we focus our gaze upon the holy loving God, allowing this vision to inform our ethical imaginations. We are also enabled to recognize our darkness and sin in the presence of divine light, thereby provoking penitence and repentance, both fundamental ingredients of real change. We also learn to receive forgiveness and grace and the spiritual empowering to move forward.

In studying Scripture we begin to learn biblical values and norms and virtues. We learn the kinds of speech and behavior that are holy and those that are not.

Intentional strategies of re-forming habits also play a role—making a decision to avoid the well-worn sledge tracks down the snowy hill, the tracks that tend to keep us repeating the same old route again and again.

This is about picking new directions and beginning the hard work of forging new pathways. For instance, intentionally avoiding situations in which you are likely to gossip, or, if they are unavoidable, biting your tongue and refusing to gossip when the opportunities arise, even if you are itching to. And if you fail, acknowledging this, repenting, and moving forward again, and again, and again until the new patterns become more and more instinctive. Holiness as a lifestyle is not something that happens in the blinking of an eye—bodies and minds need retraining.

All this must be done in community as we travel the road together, encouraging and correcting one another in love. And it must begin in catechesis.

Catechesis Is Learning to Interpret Our Culture through the Biblical Story and to Inhabit It with Holiness

The *Epistle to Diognetus* says of Christians: "They live in their own countries, but only as resident aliens. They have a share in everything as citizens, and endure everything as foreigners. Every foreign land is their fatherland, and yet for them every fatherland is a foreign land" (*Diogn.* 5). Christians have to live *in* the world yet remain not *of* the world. This requires discernment to see behind the glittering projections of the good life that we are constantly exposed to. Christians need to be taught how to see with subversive gospel eyes: to discern the values that underlie various social, cultural, economic, and political institutions and practices, to be able to deconstruct adverts, interpret pop culture, question the unquestionable assumptions underlying the world as given.

This is a difficult lifelong process of discernment and communal self-reflection, for there is nothing so hard to see as one's own unquestioned assumptions. Nevertheless, starting on that journey is important and it requires both training and the insight of a community of fellow-questers. Catechesis is the time to begin that voyage.

Catechesis Involves "Exorcism"

All of us can face the classic temptations of money, sex, and power. For many people these can be more than temptations, becoming, to one degree or another, addictions. Perhaps more than any time in history people—especially in the consumerist West—have been trained to be insatiably addicted to acquiring more and more "stuff." This is not an innocent pastime but a compulsion that needs breaking.

For the early church exorcism from demonic powers was a normal part of the process of catechesis and preparing people to be united to Christ in baptism. Many of us are enslaved in one way or another to things from which we need to be set free. Catechesis is the time to start dealing with such issues—learning to name these compulsions as idols, to renounce them, and to receive prayer and mentoring.

Catechesis Is Learning to Engage in God's Mission

Mission is first and foremost *God's* mission for the sake of the world: *God* is the one who sends and *God* is the one who is sent into the world. Thus Christians claim that the Father loved the world so much that he sent his one and only Son and then, through the Son, he poured out the Spirit. This was so that God could reconcile the world to himself and lead creation into resurrection life, new creation. That, in broadest terms, is mission.

But God's mission has a church that serves as the body of Christ to and for the world. So while "God was in Christ reconciling the world to himself" that church is called to proclaim, "Be reconciled to God." That church is called to work in the world so that God's kingdom may come on earth as in heaven. And mission is as broad as God's work in restoring creation. It includes evangelism, but far exceeds it.

Catechesis is where people are introduced to the breadth of God's mission, the work of the Spirit-filled church in being a medium of that mission, and the multiple ways in which the church can fulfill it. It is also the place in which individuals are encouraged to start participating in God's mission in exploratory ways.

Catechesis Involves Increasing Participation in the Faith Community

We humans are relational creatures and we crave communion. But in our increasingly mobile societies local communities change through immigration and emigration at a far more rapid pace than in the past. This lack of stability makes building deep, lasting relationships more and more difficult. Added to that is the way in which changing patterns of work, family life, entertainment, and the rise of the internet mean that more and more people spend more and more time at home; and when we socialize we increasingly do so remotely. Through social networks we can be together alone.

But while online communities are of value, they are ever-shifting, loose networks of relationships that can easily tend toward superficiality. They work best if we recognize them for what they are and don't look to them to fulfill our needs for intimacy. They can support embodied, face-to-face relationships in helpful ways—helping us to keep in touch more easily—but what they can never do is to *substitute* for embodied community. Man cannot live by web alone.

Here the church faces a challenge and an opportunity. Community is essential to the church—we are the family of God and meaningful inter-relationship is part of the heart of being church. But being community requires time spent together, both in gathered worship and in working, resting, and playing. It requires growing intimacy and openness and trust. This is a major challenge in the West where people are resource rich but time poor. It requires intentionality and commitment and sacrifice. And there are no shortcuts, for the kind of communities we are speaking of here *cannot* be lived online. They demand embodied presence.

The church also faces an opportunity here. Robert Putnam observed in his book *Bowling Alone* that over the past few decades in America there has been a significant drop in participation in organizations, churches, social clubs (reading groups, sports clubs, interest groups), political engagement, and the like. People are less involved with their families, their local communities, and even meet friends less frequently. Yet people still yearn for community and intimacy. "Social life is disappointing. The very franticness of attempts to reestablish community and festival, by partying, by group, by club, by touristy Mardi Gras, is the best evidence of the loss of true community and festival and of the loneliness of self, stranded as it is as an unspeakable consciousness in a world from which it perceives itself as somehow estranged, stranded even within its own body, with which it sees no clear connection."[6] We look to technology to provide solutions but the best it can provide are pale imitations of closeness. The church is called to be a truly human community and, when being true to this calling, offers what many people are looking for—genuine community.

Of course, while many postmodern people desire the intimacy of real community and speak of the importance of relationality it remains the case that when the rubber hits the road the costs are often too high. We want

---

6. Percy, *Lost in the Cosmos* (1983), 180.

intimacy but we want it *now* and on *our* terms! And if we cannot get that then we will go somewhere else where we can—after all, the consumer is king! Being part of a Christian community is not easy for Westerners for we have been deformed into those who consume relationships for our gratification. There are a host of virtues that need to be developed—love, joy, peace, patience, kindness, goodness, faithfulness, gentleness, and self-control—and there are many hard lessons that we need to learn about humility, apologizing, forgiveness, and sticking with people when they let us down.

Catechesis is where this starts. Catechetical groups need to form into committed small groups that support each other and catechists also need to be gradually introduced into the life of the main church community.

A Word about the Christian Year and Spiritual Formation

Not all Christians celebrate the Christian Year, and those that do will not all celebrate it according to the same pattern. Nevertheless, it remains the case that all the historic churches—Catholic, Orthodox, and Protestant— do organize the feasts and fasts of the year around the story of Jesus. All of them celebrate Christmas and Easter, Christ's birth and death-burial-resurrection, as the twin hubs around which the year moves; all of them mark what the West calls Advent (anticipating the first and second comings of the Messiah), Epiphany (Christ's manifestation in the coming of the Magi or in Christ's baptism), Lent (Christ's testing in the wilderness), and Pentecost (the giving of the Spirit).

To many evangelical Christians this all seems mere "religion" with little life. On the contrary, the Christian Year offers a real Christ-centered alternative to the secularized view of time as, to borrow a phrase from Arnold Toynbee, just "one damn thing after another." In Christendom time was not simply linear, with *a* followed by *b* followed by *c* and so on *ad infinitum*. Rather there was linear time but there were also what philosopher Charles Taylor calls "higher time." This was a sacred time that encompassed but transcended linear time. And the sacred moments of the Christian Year belong to this higher time, providing access beyond the mundane. When twenty-first-century Christians celebrate Easter they are, in one very real sense, closer *in time* to Christians in the sixth century celebrating Easter than they are to people in ordinary time the previous year. The Christian Year compels the very shape of time itself to bow the knee to Christ. It teaches us to submit to the rhythms of our own lives to the story of Jesus, that our time is not our own to determine. It also takes us through seasons of hope and penitence, of feasting and fasting, of joy and sorrow. It refuses to allow us to neglect one part of the Christian story and to focus entirely on another, keeping us from getting unbalanced. The Christian Year, observed with integrity, is spiritually formative.

One of the sad things about churches that do not observe the Christian Year is that, although they often claim to avoid the pitfalls of the endless repetition of the spirals of sacred time, in actual fact they are vastly more repetitive and predictable. Indeed, it is often the case that any single meeting in any year could be interchanged with any other and nobody would notice the difference. Every gathering is generic praise + praise + praise followed by preaching on whatever topic the preacher feels led to speak about. One danger here is that you can go for years without seasons of repentance or without considering Christ's ascension or the incarnation or whatever. Unbalance is lurking in the wings. Another danger here is that we do not respect the ebb and flow of the seasons of life, the need to give space for different patterns of relating to the divine. Instead we simply enact a religious version of secular time—one blessed thing after another.

Now celebrating the Christian Year is no guarantee of spiritual life—there are far too many counter-examples to believe that. Nevertheless, we would urge that it is a wonderful gift bequeathed to us by the church of the past that provides a rich resource for remembering our future.

We are not suggesting that one *needs* the Christian Year in order to nurture a balanced spirituality—churches that do not follow it can be wonderful communities of disciples—but we do think that the price of this time-as-a-blank-slate approach, with its inherent dangers, is eternal vigilance.

The Practice of Catechesis

Alan Kreider suggests that we need to get serious about catechesis: "As we prepare candidates for baptism today, let the preparations last not six weeks but sixty weeks, or even ninety weeks, which is only half of what the *Apostolic Tradition* specifies."[7] He asks, "Can we, in our culture, become disciples of Jesus easily, quickly, without mentors, without sacrifice?"[8] Catechesis, he suggests, would have various methods of delivery: formal teaching sessions,

7. Kreider, "Baptism and Catechesis" (2007), 177.
8. Ibid., 202.

engagement in regular practical action (such as working with the homeless, prison visiting, or helping at a hospice, evangelism), one-to-one mentoring, "exorcism," and increasing participation in the main church community.

If we build Christian communities that take catechesis and ongoing spiritual formation seriously we will have gone a long way toward creating coherent plausibility shelters for the Christian imagination that enable the church to be a gospel-shaped community in the midst of a world with very different ambitions.

9

Deep Church

A Eucharistic Community

IN THIS FINAL CHAPTER we shall pull together some threads by exploring deep church as a eucharistic community, for in the Eucharist right belief, right worship, and right practice embrace.

The Mysterious Case of the Missing Eucharist

Whocarist? McEucharist

"There would seem to be little doubt that neglect of the Lord's Supper or the Eucharist is one of the hallmarks of contemporary evangelicalism."[1] It is the secret confession of many evangelicals that Holy Communion has been a big disappointment. It is celebrated because Jesus instituted it, but for many, in their more honest moments, having a sip of wine and a tiny piece of bread hardly amount to the highlight of the week, either in culinary or spiritual terms. It is done to remember the death of Christ but for many evangelicals we can do that in other, more interesting, ways—we remembered the death of Christ when we sing songs of worship and when we pray; the bread and wine don't seem to add much to that.

Many evangelical churches manage to get by without Holy Communion most of the time—more whocarist? than Eucharist. For instance, we know of churches that have gone for over a year without celebrating

1. Truman, "The Incarnation and the Lord's Supper" (2003), 185.

Communion and without even realizing that they had done so. We know of other evangelical churches where people would turn up on a Sunday and then someone would remember at the last minute that it was a Communion week so they'd rush off to get bread and wine.

We know of many evangelical churches where the Eucharist, when it is celebrated, is shoehorned into a meeting just after the "worship" time and just before the sermon (neither of which seem to link to it in any meaningful way). This is fast food worship; welcome to McEucharist. All this says a lot about how undervalued Communion is. We may utter fine words about the Lord's Supper but our actions often reveal that for many of us it is something of an afterthought rather than the climax of an encounter with Christ.

That the Eucharist is peripheral to the spiritual life of many evangelicals should strike us as odd. Jesus himself gave this meal to the church and from the start most Christians have made Holy Communion the *center* of their worship. So how is it that so many evangelicals imagine that they can come to the heart of worship without it? How has it come to seem like a distraction from the *real* business of worship? The answer lies, in large part, in theology. While most believers are not theologians, any Christian who takes Communion has some view about what is going on when they do it and it is in those ideas where the problem resides.

Zwingli and the Theological Road to McEucharist

Ulrich Zwingli (1484–1531), the Swiss Reformer, was very influenced by Renaissance humanism with its aversion to scholasticism and its adulation of reason. He wanted none of the mystical eucharistic hocus pocus he perceived in medieval Catholicism. Zwingli understood the sacraments to be demonstrations of allegiance; oaths or pledges by the believer to other believers. For him the "is" in "this *is* my body" means "signifies" rather than "is identical with." When someone holds up a drawing of their mother and says, "This *is* my mother," they do not mean that the drawing is literally identical with their mother but that it represents their mother; so too, according to Zwingli, with Communion. Taking this idea he argued against the real presence of Christ in the Eucharist in his treatise *On the Lord's Supper* (1526).

Zwingli saw Christ's death as the victory battle over sin and thus as the foundational event for the church's identity. The Eucharist, he maintained, was simply a *memorial* of the death of Christ, a *commemoration* of that battle. As such it is no more necessary for Christ to be present in the Eucharist and for Christ's death to be "repeated" in it than for the battle of Nahenfels to be reenacted in order to be commemorated. So the Eucharist is more about the *absence* of Christ than about his presence. Christ's body is currently at the right hand of the Father in heaven and is absent from the earth. Communion is simply what Christians do "until he comes." Thus Christ is present in the Lord's Supper *only* in the sense that he is remembered in the hearts of those who participate.

Zwingli's theology reflects a deep dualism. He thought that no physical element can affect the soul, but only God working directly in his sovereign grace. Consequently the signs (bread and wine) and what they signify (body and blood) must be *held apart*. The sign merely helps the mind to rise above the realm of the senses to the spiritual reality signified.

The historical influence of Renaissance humanism and Enlightenment rationalism on evangelicalism has tended to favor non-mystical views of the Lord's Supper. "Sacramental realism does not comport easily with modern rationality."[2] Thus Zwingli's view seems to be the default position of many evangelicals. This is perhaps because it is a simple view that is easy to understand and that avoids Catholic alternatives (something that evangelicals have been historically concerned to do).

However, it is our contention that Zwingli's understanding of Communion actually *undermines* the importance of the meal Christ gave us. Why? Because it is perfectly possible to remember Christ's death for us and to pledge allegiance to him *without taking Communion*. Communion simply becomes one way of achieving a goal that can be achieved in other ways. And after all, isn't it the attitude of the heart that really matters—the outer rituals are just secondary fluff? So evangelicals carry on breaking bread because of Jesus' command to do so but deep down in their hearts perhaps the suspicion is that Holy Communion is *non-essential*.

Deep Church: Recovering from Zwingli

"The real voyage of discovery consists not in seeking new landscapes, but in having new eyes."[3] There is a tendency in charismatic circles to look for

2. Clapp, *Tortured Wonders* (2004), 99.

3. This is actually a paraphrase of Marcel Proust (1871–1922): "The only true voyage of discovery . . . would be not to visit strange lands but to possess other eyes, to behold the universe through the eyes of another" (*The Captive and the Fugitive* [1996], chap. 2).

the next trendy spiritual buzz in exotic new places—in new landscapes. We want to invite you to look again with new eyes at the divine gift that is *already in our midst.* The old friend we thought we knew turns out to be stranger and yet more wonderful than we could have imagined. Do we dare to see this old landscape with new eyes? To see that this normal, "mundane" practice of Holy Communion is actually anything but mundane. To do this we need to get over Zwingli.

Recovering Real Presence

THE SPIRITUALITY OF THE PHYSICAL WORLD

To appreciate real presence we need to lay a little groundwork. Often we tend to think of the world divided into two kinds of stuff—physical stuff like rocks and spiritual stuff like angels. Physical stuff, we suppose, is not so important and spiritual stuff is very important. So we draw a neat division in creation with the less important stuff being things like mountains, trees, human bodies, eating, running, and the like. The more important stuff is things like human souls, angels, prayer, thinking, Bible reading, and so on. We want real encounters with God to be spiritual encounters that bypass all the physical side of the world—direct Spirit-to-spirit communication. Clearly if that is what we are after then Holy Communion is just too physical and ordinary. It includes mundane things like bread and like wine—about the most common kinds of foods you could get in ancient Israel. There is also the whole physicality of taste, texture, smell, and color. It includes bodies doing certain things and saying certain words. It is multisensory and profoundly physical and a big disappointment for all those who think physical stuff is just not spiritual enough.

We have some good news. God made this good creation in all its materiality and all its spirituality and you cannot divide the two. You cannot have a pure spiritual encounter with God—that would not be a *human* encounter at all. Humans are *embodied* creatures because that is how God made us. God's spiritual encounters with us always have a physical dimension (even the deep spiritual zingy feelings you may get sometimes are connected to things happening in your brain). Our problem is that we have too low a view of just how spiritual the physical universe is. But just think a moment about how God encounters people in the Bible.

- Noah: the rains came down and the floods came up

- Elijah: the rain does not come down and the flood does not come up.

- Moses: finds a weird burning bush up on a mountain

- Israelites: he sends a wind and the sea parts

- Josiah: through the words of a book read to him

- Joshua: Israel's armies win in battle

- Zedekiah: Israel's armies lose in battle

All of this is the meat and bone of the way God engages with his people and all of it is spiritual but all of it is *mediated through the physical world that God has made.* And for a Christian the ultimate proof of this has to be the Christmas story. Jesus is the supreme revelation of God according to the NT. Through Jesus, God is acting in the world in the most astonishing way ever. But he does so *through the physical humanity of Jesus.* God is encountered in Jesus' actions and Jesus' words. You don't see God "raw" as it were (no one has ever seen God). You see God in and through a physical human being. The point is that God meets us primarily in and through the physicality of his creation.

We are embodied creatures not ghosts trapped in meat machines. So the way that we know things—the world around us and even God— is embodied. Holy Communion is a key Christian way of knowing God carefully crafted for creatures such as ourselves. So let's acknowledge and celebrate all the physicality of it—the smells, the textures, the tastes, the sights, the sounds, the ways we move our bodies as we share the peace and as we reach out our hands to accept the bread and wine. These things are not distractions from the spiritual but, if we attend rightly to them, a means of discerning the spiritual.

> A man that looks on glass
> On it may stay his eye
> Or if he pleaseth, through it pass
> And then the heaven espy.[4]

This insight is simple and obvious yet so often ignored. But unless we grasp the spiritual potential of the physical stuff of the world—of ordinary bread and wine for instance—we will never appreciate the spiritual power of Holy Communion.

---

4. George Herbert, "Teach Me, My God and King."

Some of the ancient British Christians used to speak of certain places being "thin places." By this they meant that the veil between heaven and earth is thinner and more transparent in those places. One could sense there the presence of Holiness—of God's reality. We wish to suggest that understanding the spiritual potential of the material allows us to see how Holy Communion can be such a "thin place."

THE EARLY CHURCH'S UNDERSTANDING OF THE EUCHARIST

> Jesus said to them, "Truly, truly, I say to you, unless you eat the flesh of the Son of Man and drink his blood, you have no life in you. Whoever feeds on my flesh and drinks my blood has eternal life, and I will raise him up on the last day. For my flesh is true food, and my blood is true drink. Whoever feeds on my flesh and drinks my blood abides in me, and I in him. As the living Father sent me, and I live because of the Father, so whoever feeds on me, he also will live because of me. This is the bread that came down from heaven, not like the bread the fathers ate, and died. Whoever feeds on this bread will live forever." (John 6:53–58)

> The cup of blessing that we bless, is it not a participation in the blood of Christ? The bread that we break, is it not a participation in the body of Christ? (1 Cor 10:16)

Fundamental to recovering deep church, we maintain, is restoring the ancient Christian notion of the real presence of Jesus in Holy Communion. Ignatius of Antioch (c. AD 110) speaks of those who hold aloof from the Eucharist and prayer "because they do not confess that the Eucharist is the Flesh of our Savior Jesus Christ" (Ign. *Smyrn.* 7). Justin Martyr, writing in about AD 150, said, "as we have been taught, the food which has been made into the Eucharist by the Eucharistic prayer set down by him, and by the change of which our flesh and blood is nourished, is both the flesh and blood of that incarnate Jesus" (*1 Apol.* 66). And here is Cyril of Jerusalem (c. AD 350):

> Therefore, it is with complete assurance that we receive the bread and wine as the body and blood of Christ. His body is given to us under the symbol of bread, and his blood is given to us under the symbol of wine, in order to make us by receiving them one body and blood with him. Having his body and blood in our members, we become bearers of Christ and sharers, as Saint Peter says, in the

divine nature. . . . Do not, then, regard the Eucharistic elements
as ordinary bread and wine: they are in fact the body and blood
of the Lord, as he himself has declared. Whatever your senses tell
you, be strong in faith. You have been taught and are firmly convinced that what looks and tastes like bread and wine is not bread
and wine but the body and blood of Christ. . . . Strengthen your
heart then by receiving this bread as spiritual bread, and bring joy
to the face of your souls. (*Myst.* 22)

It is important to understand Cyril's language of symbolism here. Paul
Bradshaw notes that "in the ancient world a sign or symbol was not thought
of as being something quite different from the reality which it represented,
but on the contrary was understood as participating in some way in the
reality itself."[5] This is why Cyril can speak in the passage above of the eucharistic elements as symbols and as "in fact the body and blood of the Lord."

Ancient eucharistic prayers also reflect this theology of real presence.
Here is a prayer attributed to the fourth-century bishop Sarapion: "Let your
holy Word come on this bread, O God of truth, that the bread may become
body of the Word; and on this cup, that the cup may become the blood of
the Truth."[6] But from the fourth century on the dominant prayer, especially
in the East, became the epiclesis, the invocation of the Holy Spirit to come
consecrate the elements and/or the congregation. The prayer of Addai
and Mari, a Syrian epiclesis says, "May your Holy Spirit, Lord, come and
rest on this offering of your servants, and bless and sanctify it."[7] And Basil
writes, "And we, sinners and unworthy and wretched, pray you our God,
in adoration that in the good pleasure of your goodness your Holy Spirit
may descend upon us and upon these gifts that have been set before you,
and may sanctify them and show them forth as holy of holies."[8] Theodore
of Mopsuestia tells of how the bishop prays "that the Holy Spirit may come
and that grace may descend from on high on to the bread and wine . . . so
showing us that the memorial of immortality is truly the body and blood of
our Lord" (*Bap.* 5.12). And strongest of all, John Chrysostom: "[W]e pray
and beseech and entreat you, send down your Holy Spirit on us and on
these gifts set forth; and make this bread the precious body of your Christ,
changing it by your Holy Spirit, Amen; and that which is in this cup the

5. Bradshaw, *Early Christian Worship* (1996), 59.

6. Jasper and Cummings, eds., *Prayers of the Eucharist* (1985), 78–79.

7. Ibid., 43. See also Cummings, *Eucharist and Ecumenism* (2013), chap. 5.

8. Jasper and Cummings, eds., *Prayers of the Eucharist* (1985), 71 (slightly modified
by Bradshaw in *Early Christian Worship* [1996], 61–62).

precious blood of your Christ, changing it by your Holy Spirit, Amen."[9] The Holy Spirit is absolutely essential to Holy Communion. It is the Holy Spirit who thins the veil between heaven and earth. "The Spirit makes the crucified and risen Christ really present to us in the eucharistic meal."[10] However we wish to think about it, the truth is that Christ's body is in heaven but is *spiritually present* in Communion *by the Spirit*.

Thus we need to receive the elements aright. Cyril of Jerusalem expressed it thusly, "Do not have your wrists extended or your fingers spread, but making your left hand a throne for the right, for it is about to receive a king, and cupping your palm, receive the body of Christ" (*Myst.* 5.21).

The church did not feel the need to explain exactly how it could be that the bread and wine were the body and blood of Christ, though they were clear that it was not a crass eating of physical flesh and blood. Cyril, for instance, said that the revulsion of the Jews in John 6 with regard to Jesus' words about eating his flesh and drinking his blood was based on a misunderstanding: for they did not interpret the words "in a spiritual way" and thus mistakenly thought "the Savior wished them to practice cannibalism" (*Myst.* 22).

But Christ is not only the sustenance at this meal, he is the host. One of the first names that Christians gave to the Eucharist was "the Lord's Supper" (1 Cor 11:20). It is the Lord's Supper because we remember *him* but even more importantly it is the Lord's Supper because the *Lord Jesus himself is the host* of the meal. In the fourth century Basil of Caesarea said that the one who takes Communion "must believe that he duly takes and receives it from the hand that first gave it [i.e., Jesus' hand]" (*ep.* 93). Jesus prepares the meal and offers it to us. He invites us to share in it. He welcomes us to have fellowship or communion with him over this meal. Jesus calls us to eat with him and to do so not as individuals alone together like customers in McDonald's but as a family at table. It really is a meal of "Holy *Communion*."

Versions of Real Presence

The Western church gradually developed an account of the metaphysics of real presence, which was formally adopted in 1215 at the Fourth Lateran Council and has been official Catholic teaching to this day. According to this account "the body and blood of Christ are truly contained in the

9. Ibid., 133.

10. World Council of Churches, *Baptism, Eucharist, and Ministry* (1982), 13.

sacrament of the altar under the forms of bread and wine, the bread being transubstantiated into the body and the wine into the blood by divine
power." At the moment when the priest consecrates the bread and wine it
literally becomes the body and blood of Christ. More precisely, the essential
substance of the bread and wine were metaphysically transformed into the
body and blood of Christ but the *accidental properties* of the bread and wine
(the taste, texture, smell, sight) remained those of bread and wine. So what
remains after the priestly consecration looks, feels, smells, and tastes like
bread and wine *but in fact* it has been changed by a divine miracle into the
actual body and blood of Jesus. This view is known as transubstantiation.

Protestants universally rejected transubstantiation. For some, such
as Zwingli, this also meant rejecting real presence and, as we have seen,
many Protestants have followed on his coat tails. The Reformers thought
the Catholic teaching that the Mass was a sacrifice undermined the fundamental once-and-for-all nature of Jesus' death. They reasoned that if the
priest literally sacrificed Jesus again week by week then the gospel itself was
threatened because Jesus' death was declared inadequate and in need of
regular supplementing. Of course, everything depends on how the teaching of the Mass as a sacrifice was understood. It was never the intention of
the Catholic Church to deny the adequacy of Calvary, and contemporary
Catholic theology is very clear that the Mass is a Holy Sacrifice because it
makes present the one sacrifice of Christ the Savior. The Eucharist in no
way replaces, adds to, or improves on the cross. Rather, it is a means of *real
participation* in that once-for-all sacrifice. So in our view transubstantiation, whether we think it a helpful account of real presence or not, does not
have the fearful consequences the Reformers worried about.

Furthermore, even if transubstantiation is problematic, real presence does not depend on it. Luther and Calvin managed to hold on to
the doctrine of real presence, albeit in very different ways, while rejecting
transubstantiation. Luther maintained that Christ was *bodily present* in the
Eucharist and that those who partook of it received his actual body and
blood. "On this we take our stand, and we also believe and teach that in the
supper we eat and take to ourselves Christ's body truly and physically."[11] He
took the words "this is my body" literally and ferociously opposed Zwingli's
claim that the eucharistic elements are merely symbolic. What Luther
objected to in transubstantiation was *not* the claim that Christ was really
present in the elements but the explanation as to *how* Christ was present. To

11. Luther, *That These Words of Christ Still Stand Firm against the Fanatics* (1959), in
LW 37:28.

Luther the bread and wine remain (*contra* Rome) but they are accompanied by the body and blood of Christ, which are present "in," "with," and "under" the bread and wine.[12]

Calvin held that believers really do feed on Christ's body and blood in the Eucharist (*contra* Zwingli) but in a *spiritual* manner not a physical one (*contra* Rome and Luther). It was never the real presence of Christ in Holy Communion that Calvin disputed but the *manner* of that presence. The sacrament is a real means of grace by which Christ communicates himself to his people.

Calvin supported Zwingli's claim that the signs (bread and wine) and the things signified (body and blood) must be recognized as distinct but they are not, he insisted, able to be separated. As Christ's human and divine natures are distinct but inseparable so too we must not posit a division between the physical signs of bread and wine and the spiritual realities that they convey even though they are distinct. The Eucharist is both symbolic *and* real for it mediates what it signifies.

The *Holy Spirit* is the bond of connection uniting the physical symbols and the spiritual reality. However, Calvin's understanding of what the Spirit does is quite new and worthy of consideration. Roman Catholic theology and Orthodox theology also stress the key place of the Spirit in the transformation of the elements into the body and blood of Christ (reflected in the epiclesis prayer). But Calvin does not think that the Spirit brings Christ's body down to earth. Rather, the Spirit elevates believers into heavenly places where Christ is. The Spirit enables us to ascend to him (spiritually) and thus to feed on him (spiritually) as we partake of the elements.

> But if we are lifted up to heaven with our eyes and minds to seek Christ there in the glory of his Kingdom, so under the symbol of bread we shall be fed by his body, [and] under the symbol of wine we shall separately drink his blood to enjoy him at last in his wholeness. For though he has taken his flesh away, and in the

12. In our opinion Luther's account of how this is so is deeply problematic, being based upon a misuse of the classical doctrine of the communication of idioms. Luther thought that because Christ's divine and human natures were united in one person then the properties of each nature applied to the other. So Christ's *human nature is omnipresent* because his divine nature is. Consequently Christ's *humanity* fills the universe, and thus the eucharistic elements. But the classical account of the communication of idioms was very careful to keep the divine and human natures distinct. What it maintained was that the divine Logos was the single subject of all the properties of the divine and human natures, not that the properties of each nature applied to the other nature. That is why Zwingli and Calvin disputed Luther's view of the Eucharist.

body has ascended into heaven, yet he sits at the right hand of the Father. (*Institutes* 4.17.18)

So Christ's human body is limited to heaven and never leaves heaven. But the Spirit comes down on us and mystically lifts us up where we spiritually commune with Christ. Quite how the Spirit does this is a mystery: "What then, our mind does not comprehend, let faith conceive: that the Spirit truly unites things separated in space" (*Institutes* 7.17.10). This echoes the Orthodox understanding of the Eucharist as *mysterion* (mystery) and is reminiscent of John of Damascus's words, "[I]f you inquire as to how this takes place, it is enough for you to know that it is effected by the Holy Spirit" (*Ortho.* 4.13). The Spirit is active, feeding believers by nourishing, sustaining, and increasing the mystical union with Christ as they eat the bread and drink the wine.

That the doctrine of real presence does not depend on the theology of transubstantiation is also revealed by the fact that that Eastern Orthodox church, for whom real presence is critical, never embraced it. For the Orthodox, the Eucharist "is strictly understood as the real presence of Christ, his true body and blood mystically present in the bread and wine, which are offered to the Father in Jesus' name and consecrated by the divine Spirit of God."[13]

The Orthodox resist any attempt to set what is "real" in opposition to what is "symbolic" or "mystical." So to say, like Zwingli, that the Eucharist is a symbol of Christ but Christ is not really present in it strikes them as an unhelpful, reductionistic distinction. All of reality is both symbolic and mystical. Sym-bolic literally means "to bring together into one." In the Eucharist the bread and wine are brought into union with the real body and blood. They are understood to be the genuine body and blood of Christ because they symbolize God's true and genuine presence.

Our point here is not to arbitrate between the diverse Christian accounts of real presence—from pious agnosticism to transubstantiation to Luther to Calvin—but simply to emphasize that the Christian churches have classically affirmed the doctrine as central to understanding the Eucharist. Holy Communion *is* a symbol but never *just* a symbol.

---

13. Website of the Orthodox Church in America. For more on Orthodoxy and the Eucharist, see Wybrew, *The Orthodox Liturgy* (1992).

REAL LIFE-GIVING PRESENCE

The importance of real presence is that the meal itself, according to the tradition, is a means by which we participate in the eternal life in Christ— "Whoever feeds on my flesh and drinks my blood has eternal life" (John 6:54). Jesus *himself* is the spiritual "bread" we "eat" and the "wine" we "drink." It was the unanimous view in the early centuries of the church that taking Holy Communion with faith brought the resurrection life of Christ to those who took it. When you eat or drink something it enters right into the depths of you—it brings you life—it becomes part of you. The food is digested and there is no longer a dividing line between your body and the food—"you are what you eat." Jesus speaks of drinking his blood and eating his flesh as a metaphor for taking his very life deep into our own spiritual lives by faith. We are united with him—his life becomes our life. That's what it's all about. This is "spiritual food and drink" (*Did.* 10). Some even see it as bringing life to our mortal bodies now, anticipating the resurrection body: Justin Martyr speaks of how "our flesh and blood is nourished" by partaking in the flesh and blood of Jesus in Communion (*1 Apol.* 66) and Irenaeus says, "our bodies, when they receive the Eucharist, are no longer corruptible, having the hope of the resurrection to eternity" (*Haer.* 4.18).

Once you start thinking in these terms Communion is suddenly something far more significant than an optional addition to a meeting for a bit of variety every now and again. Once you start looking in this way it becomes far clearer why most Christians past and present have honored it as a divine gift.

Right Belief and Eucharist

The Eucharist bears within itself the marks of the whole biblical metanarrative, from creation to new creation. Like the hub at the center of a bicycle wheel, where all the spokes meet, Communion is that sacred center that gathers together Christian doctrine. Thus to participate in Holy Communion is to practice "right belief"; to engage—often without realizing it— with the breadth of Christian theology.

Creation

Let's start at the very beginning (a very good place to start). The use of bread and wine—representing both the natural world (grain, water, and grapes) and its human cultivation and transformation—makes the very physicality of the Eucharist an affirmation and celebration of creation in all its spiritual materiality.

In the second century, Irenaeus opposed gnostics who believed that physical reality (the flesh) is incapable of receiving divine life (in the resurrection of the body). He uses a common Christian understanding of the Eucharist to do so: if the bread and wine are transformed into the body and blood of the Lord then dualism in theology and the rejection of physicality must cease.

> He [Christ] has acknowledged the cup (which is a part of the creation) as His own blood, from which he bedews our blood; and the bread (also part of the creation) He has established as his own body, from which he gives increase to our own bodies. When, therefore, the mingled cup and the manufactured bread receives the Word of God, and the Eucharist of the blood and the body of Christ is made . . . how can they affirm that the flesh is incapable of receiving the gift of God, which is eternal life . . . (*Haer.* 5.2.2–3)

By making the centerpiece of worship such an embodied engagement with God the church takes a doxological stand against all that denigrates God's world or that seeks to bypass it in the pursuit of the divine.

Fall

The Lord's Supper does not commemorate sin but it does presuppose it. The meal offers healing and forgiveness and life to those who are wounded, broken, sinful, and spiritually dead. It is preceded by confession of sin and repentance and partaken in as a means of grace. By being "for the forgiveness of sins" (Matt 26:28) it also serves as a constant reminder of the story of the Fall and our need of grace.

Israel and the Exodus

The Lord's Supper was instituted by Jesus at his last Passover meal with his disciples. The bread and the wine were elements of the traditional Jewish Passover, given a transformed meaning by Jesus. And the echo of Passover continues in the meal. In Christian typological understandings of the Passover Christ is the lamb sacrificed (1 Cor 5:7) but also the bread is his body and the wine his blood. The Passover celebrates Israel's exodus from Egypt and the Eucharist celebrates, among other things, the exodus of God's people from sin and death. Eucharist is not a Passover meal—the evidence we have suggests that Christians never treated it as a once-a-year celebration at Passover time—but it still bears in its body the genetic inheritance of its parent. It still speaks of an exodus for the people of God from slavery and of redemption by the blood of a sacrificial lamb.

Jesus told his followers to eat the meal together "in remembrance of me" (Luke 22:19). This too is an echo of Passover. God had said in Exodus 12:14, "This day shall be a remembrance for you." But the kind of "remembrance" God had in mind was no mere Zwinglian thinking-about-a-once-for-all-event-long-ago. During the Passover meal the exodus story is retold and the meal enables each generation of Jews to *participate* in the ancient story as if they were the ones being delivered from Egypt. In the meal they symbolically share in the sufferings of their ancestors and symbolically partake in the salvation experienced. The past event becomes a present experience through the ritual of the meal. This is remembrance by participation. For the Jews who share in the meal they are those who Jehovah rescued from Egypt. Here is how the Jewish Mishnah puts it: "In every generation a man must so regard himself as if he came forth out of Egypt" (*m. Pesaḥ* 10.4). This is the kind of remembrance Christ calls us to: "As we hear the story of the first supper over and over in our worship it becomes our story, our memory, we were there; . . . this remembering at the Lord's Supper [is] owning the stories as our own."[14] In Eucharist we "remember" by immersing the stories of our lives in the story of our Lord.

Incarnation

Ignatius of Antioch's comment about those who stand back from the Eucharist "because they do not confess that the Eucharist is the Flesh of our

---

14. Vander Zee, *Christ, Baptism and the Lord's Supper* (2004), 149.

Savior Jesus Christ which suffered for our sins and which the Father raised by his goodness" (Ign. *Smyrn.* 7.1) suggests that the use of realistic language when speaking of the bread and wine "may have arisen to counteract heretical claims that Christ was not truly human and did not really suffer and die on the cross."[15] Certainly the church came to recognize orthodox claims about the incarnation as connected with real presence in the Eucharist. Justin Martyr in about AD 150 wrote:

> For not as common bread nor as common drink do we receive these; but since Jesus Christ our Savior was made incarnate by the word of God and had both flesh and blood for our salvation, so too, as we have been taught, the food which has been made into the Eucharist by the Eucharistic prayer set down by him, and by the change of which our flesh and blood is nourished, is both the flesh and blood of that incarnate Jesus. (*1 Apol.* 66)

The doctrine of the incarnation—that the divine Logos can be encountered in physical stuff—is part of the very fabric of the Eucharist.

Atonement

Perhaps the most obvious aspect of the Eucharist is that those who partake in it "proclaim the Lord's death" (1 Cor 11:26). His body "given for you" and his blood "poured out for you" speak eloquently of the price paid by Jesus for the salvation of humanity (1 Cor 11:23–25). This lifeblood ritually inaugurates the eschatological new covenant promised by Jeremiah (Jer 31:31–34; Mark 14:24; Matt 26:28; Luke 22:20; 1 Cor 11:25). Historically the language of sacrifice has also been used to describe the rite[16] for it was a means of participating in the once-and-for-all sacrifice of Jesus.[17] Jesus, in Matthew's Gospel, says that his blood was "poured out for many for the forgiveness of sins" (26:28), highlighting another dimension of salvation.

Resurrection

Speaking of the epiclesis, Theodore says, "This is the moment appointed for Christ our Lord to rise from the dead and pour out his grace upon us all"

---

15. Bradshaw, *Early Christian Worship* (1996), 60.
16. Cyprian, *ep.* 63.14; Cyril of Jerusalem, *Myst.* 5.10; Gregory Nazianzen, *ep.* 171.
17. John Chrysostom, *Hom. in Heb.* 17.6.

(*Bap.* 5.11–12). Bradshaw explains, "The bread and wine which have until now symbolized the dead body of Jesus become his risen body."[18] Resurrection is represented in Holy Communion in the themes of eternal life granted to those who partake in faith and in the theme of Jesus as the host of the meal who is in heaven inviting his church to participate in his life. Eucharist makes no sense if it is simply a celebration of a dead Lord.

Ecclesiology

As we saw in chapter 7, Paul in 1 Corinthians considered the Lord's Supper to be packed full of implications for being church. "Because there is one bread, we who are many are one body, *for* we all partake of the one bread" (1 Cor 10:17). The Eucharist is about the unity of many in the one—that is, Christ; it is about catholicity. If we share in this meal, he said, then we celebrate our equality and our diversity as parts of Christ's one body (12:12–31; Rom 12:4–8). Those differences that could divide us—race, gender, and social status—are transcended in this kingdom meal. Consequently there are ways of treating each other—ways that play on the social significance of those very distinctions—that are simply incompatible with the meaning of the Supper, for they deny our new equal status in Christ (1 Cor 11:17–32).

The catholicity of the eucharistic community is, as John Zizioulas points out, a *christological* category. The church is catholic *because she is the body of Christ*. Thus,

> it is *Christ's* unity and it is *His* catholicity that the Church reveals in her being catholic. This means that her catholicity is neither an objective gift to be possessed nor an objective order to be fulfilled, but rather a *presence*, a presence which unites into a single existential reality both what is given and what is demanded, the presence of Him who sums up in Himself the community and the entire creation by His being existentially involved in both of them. The Church is catholic only by virtue of her being where His presence is.[19]

And this unifying presence of Christ in the church is realized *only* by the ongoing power of the Spirit in the community (hence the importance of the epiclesis prayer during the Eucharist).

18. Ibid., 68.
19. Zizioulas, *Being as Communion* (1997), 159–60.

John Chrysostom, in about 390, wrote, "Therefore, in order that we may become his body, not in desire only, but also in very fact, let us become commingled with that body. This, in truth, takes place by means of the food which he has given to us as a gift" (*Hom. Jo.* 46, commenting on John 6). Partaking in Holy Communion is, for Chrysostom, the means by which we are constituted in an ongoing way as Christ's one body. As such it is central and no optional extra.

The question is inevitably raised here as to whether the Eucharist makes the church or whether the church makes the Eucharist. Christians have historically taken both sides on this debate but John Zizioulas helpfully argues that the way forward is to navigate a course that embraces insights from both perspectives: *"the Church constitutes the Eucharist while being constituted by it.* Church and Eucharist are inter-dependent."[20] This is because Christ, the Son of Man, is a corporate person. "The body of Christ is not first the body of an individual Christ and *then* a community of 'many,' but simultaneously both together. . . . In the Eucharist the expression 'body of Christ' means simultaneously the body of Jesus and the body of the Church. Any separation of these two leads to the destruction of the Eucharist."[21] Theologically speaking, without the body of Christ (which is both the body of the individual man, Jesus, *and* the community that exists in him) the Eucharist is nothing—no church, no Eucharist. But by the same token the Eucharist is *the sacramental means by which* the Spirit enables us all to participate in an ongoing way in the one body of Christ (1 Cor 10:17)—no Eucharist, no church.

Finally, we may add that to be the body of *this* Lord, this cruciform Messiah, also says a lot about the nature of self-giving and suffering that are part of the nature of being church in this age. To drink Jesus' cup can have connotations of sharing in his sufferings (Matt 20:22–23). It is this dimension of the Eucharist that, as we saw in chapter 6, the Catholic Church in Chile drew on to resource their response to the torture of the Pinochet regime. Holy Communion has the resources, in the grace of God, for forming a community that is prepared to embrace suffering and self-sacrifice.

20. Zizioulas, "The Ecclesiological Presuppositions of the Holy Eucharist" (2011), 104.

21. Ibid., 105.

Eschatology

> And he said to them, "I have earnestly desired to eat this Passover
> with you before I suffer. For I tell you I will not eat it until it is ful-
> filled in the kingdom of God." And he took a cup, and when he had
> given thanks he said, "Take this, and divide it among yourselves.
> For I tell you that from now on I will not drink of the fruit of the
> vine until the kingdom of God comes." (Luke 22:15–18)

Jesus transformed his Last Supper into an anticipation of the eschatological
kingdom feast that God has prepared for his people. As Geoffrey Wainwright comments, "the eucharist is a first and partial fulfillment of the
promises of the meal of the kingdom that were given by Jesus during his
ministry and it is itself the strengthening promise of the total fulfillment in
the final consummation."[22]

Communion perfectly manifests tension that permeates the New Testament between the now and the not yet. It does reflect Christ's *absence*
from us because it is what Christians do to remember him in the time between that Last Supper and the fullness of the kingdom; it is what we do
"until he comes" (1 Cor 11:26). But it also represents his *presence (parousia)*
by his Spirit and as such it anticipates the end time wedding supper of the
Lamb. In Communion the future breaks into the present . . . but only in an
anticipatory way and not in its fullness. The future is now but not yet; the
kingdom is here but is yet to come; Christ is present but absent. To share in
this feast is therefore to participate in a meal for the time between times; to
taste the life of the age to come. Wainwright again:

> The word projection, and that in two (related) senses, may be used
> to express the relation between the final advent of Christ and the
> eucharist:
>
> (i) Christ's coming at the eucharist is a projection in the temporal
> sense that it is a "throwing forward" of Christ's final advent into
> the present. . . .
>
> (ii) Christ's coming at the eucharist is a projection of his final ad-
> vent in something like a map-maker's sense of projection. That is
> to say, it is a representation of a large reality by means of a set
> of comprehensible symbols. Only, the reality represented by the
> eucharist is not merely large but ultimate, and the relation between

22. Wainwright, *Eschatology and Eucharist* (2002), 49.

symbol and reality is not merely extrinsic and established by human convention but . . . was established by the Lord himself.[23]

Finally, we have also seen how the Eucharist anticipates our own resurrection at the end of the age, enabling Ignatius to call it "the medicine of immortality, the antidote of death" (Ign. *Eph.* 20.2). The Lord's Supper is eschatological food, a feast for the new creation.

So we see that biblical truth is inscribed into the body of the Eucharist like an intricate and subtle tattoo. To inhabit this way of worship is to situate oneself in relation to the biblical metanarrative. Once again we see that right worship is inextricable from right belief—*together* they are orthodoxy, right glory.

Indeed, not only does Eucharist embody the story of creation to new creation, it also has a fundamentally Trinitarian theology undergirding it. The church asks the Father to send his Spirit so that in the Spirit the bread and wine may be our means of communing with the Son—may be to us his body and blood—and with each other. The Father comes to us through the Son and by the Spirit. We come to the Father through the Son and by the Spirit. Without the Trinity the logic of the Eucharist collapses in on itself.

Right Practice and Eucharist

We have seen how the Lord's Supper affirms the goodness of creation in its wholeness, the nature and demands of self-giving love, of forgiveness and grace, and the diversity and solidarity of the church as the body of Christ. As such to worship in this way is to seek to live a life of cruciform Christlikeness (and if it is not then, as Paul says, it is not the Lord's Supper that you eat; 1 Cor 11:20). As Rodney Clapp observes, "the Eucharist teaches and forms the church to sacrifice itself for the sake of the world. And in that sacrifice, of course, to gain its own life."[24] So Holy Communion is ortho-praxia, right practice in terms of worship and formative for right practice in terms of Christian living.

We wish to end with some reflections on Eucharist and reconciliation from Thomas Porter, Executive Director of the United Methodist Church's Just Peace Center for Mediation and Conflict Transformation:

23. Ibid., 115–16.

24. Clapp, *Tortured Wonders* (2004), 124.

The ultimate goal of all our preparation and engagement for conflict transformation and peacebuilding is to find healing in our relationships, to flourish in community, to *be well together*. It involves more than just addressing a single conflict. It is about creating a different way of living together, a culture of justpeace. I have talked about the importance of getting people to a table where they can engage one another and work together to address the issues, the harm, and the problems that divide them. For me, that table is the Table of Holy Communion. This Table is the place, for me, where a search for a better way to deal with conflict ended. For me, this Table summarizes and empowers all that we have been discussing. This is a Table of relational healing, restorative justice, and reconciliation. At this Table we are formed into peacebuilders, ministers of reconciliation

The invitation is to those who seek to live in peace with one another. We are then sent out with the admonition to "go forth in peace." The essential power of this Table is that the One who reconciles and heals is the Host of this Table. I believe that the One in whom I have experienced God incarnate is present at all tables, but here at this Table, we recognize the Host and consciously open ourselves to this One. At the heart of the liturgy lies the good news of God's everlasting love and forgiveness in spite of our failures. At this Table we see ourselves as a forgiven people who are called to the spiritual practice of forgiveness. In fact, we are asked to work beyond forgiveness to reconciliation, as we hear the invitation to "offer one another signs of reconciliation and love." No one at this Table is unaware of the destructive conflicts in our world, in our communities, in the workplace, and in our homes. We bring all these conflicted worlds to the Table. The greatest issue of our day is how we are going to break out of the cycles of retribution and violence that are tearing our world and our relationships apart. At the Table of Holy Communion, each time we commune, we are reminded that the only way out of these cycles is through the path of forgiveness. At this Table we celebrate the defeat of the powers of retribution and violence through the word of forgiveness from the cross and through the resurrection.[25]

25. Porter, "Learning to Engage Conflict Well" (2013), 165–66.

Appendix 1

The Nicene Creed and the *Filioque*

The Two Editions of the Nicene Creed

IN ITS ORIGINAL FORM the Nicene Creed was adopted at the first ecumenical council, which met in the city of Nicea in 325. The council was convened by the Emperor Constantine to resolve the Arian controversy that was threatening to divide the church. The bishops came down against the teachings of Arius (who had taught that Jesus was not God but a creature, albeit the most exalted of all creatures). The Nicene Creed summarizes their anti-Arian presentation of the classical Christian creed.

According to tradition the second ecumenical council, held in Constantinople in 381, made some modifications to the Nicene Creed. In this book when we speak of the Nicene Creed we are actually referring to the Niceno-Constantinopolitan Creed, the version of the Nicene Creed traditionally claimed to have been modified by the Council of Constantinople in 381.[1]

1. Some scholars are inclined to think that the later version is not so much a modification of the Nicene Creed as an alternative creed that has been modified to bring it more into line with the 325 Nicene Creed. For a discussion, see Kelly, *Early Christian Creeds* (1977), chap. 10. On the one side of the debate is the tradition, which since at least the middle of the fifth century saw the Niceno-Constantinopolitan Creed as a modified version of the 325 Nicene Creed made at the second ecumenical council in 381. On the other side are scholars who see the later creed as having no connection with the council in 381. Kelly ably defends a modified version of the tradition:

> The Council of Constantinople did in fact, at some stage in its proceedings, endorse and use [the Niceno-Constantinopolitan Creed], but in doing so it did not conceive of itself as promulgating a new creed. Its sincere intention, perfectly understood by contemporary churchmen, was simply to confirm the Nicene faith. That it should do this by adopting

Appendix 1

First Council of Nicea (325)	First Council of Constantinople (381)
We believe in one God, the Father Almighty, Maker of all things visible and invisible.	We believe in one God, the Father Almighty, Maker *of heaven and earth, and* of all things visible and invisible.
And in one Lord Jesus Christ, the Son of God, begotten of the Father [the only-begotten; that is, of the essence of the Father, God of God], Light of Light, very God of very God, begotten, not made, being of one substance with the Father;	And in one Lord Jesus Christ, the *only-begotten* Son of God, begotten of the Father *before all ages*, Light of Light, very God of very God, begotten, not made, being of one substance with the Father;
By whom all things were made [both in heaven and on earth];	by whom all things were made;
Who for us men, and for our salvation, came down and was incarnate and was made man;	who for us men, and for our salvation, came down from heaven, and was incarnate *by the Holy Ghost of the Virgin Mary*, and was made man;
He suffered, and the third day he rose again, ascended into heaven;	*he was crucified for us under Pontius Pilate*, and suffered, *and was buried*, and the third day he rose again, *according to the Scriptures, and* ascended into heaven, *and sits at the right hand of the Father*;
From there he shall come to judge the living and the dead.	from there he shall come again, *with glory*, to judge the living and the dead;
	whose kingdom shall have no end.

what was really a different formula from that of Nicea may appear paradoxical to us, until we recall that at this stage importance attached to the Nicene teaching rather than to the literal wording of [the Nicene Creed]. . . . [The Niceno-Constantinopolitan Creed] was probably already in existence when the council took it up, though not necessarily in exactly the form it now wears: the fathers may well have touched it up to harmonize with their purposes. In settling upon [the Niceno-Constantinopolitan Creed] as a suitable formulary the council assumed unquestionably that it was reaffirming the Nicene teaching, but it was no doubt guided in its choice by the conviction that this particular formulation of the Nicene teaching, as modified by whatever additions it thought fit to make, was peculiarly well adapted to meet the special situation with which it was dealing. (ibid., 325)

Thus, for Kelly, the tradition is correct to associate the later creed with the Nicene Creed and also with the second ecumenical council, *even if* the modifications were not all made by the council. We have, in effect, an earlier and later version of *the same creed* and not two different creeds.

First Council of Nicea (325)	First Council of Constantinople (381)
And in the Holy Spirit.	And in the Holy Spirit, *the Lord and Giver of life, who proceeds from the Father, who with the Father and the Son together is worshiped and glorified, who spoke by the prophets.*
	In one holy catholic and apostolic church; we acknowledge one baptism for the remission of sins; we look for the resurrection of the dead, and the life of the world to come. Amen.
[But those who say: "There was a time when he was not"; and "He was not before he was made"; and "He was made out of nothing," or "He is of another substance" or "essence," or "The Son of God is created," or "changeable," or "alterable"—they are condemned by the holy catholic and apostolic church.]	

Italicized words were added in the 381 version of the Creed

Words in brackets were dropped in the 381 version of the Creed

After Nicea debate arose about the deity of the Spirit and it became important to clarify that issue. So Nicea's simple "and in the Holy Spirit" was expanded to make clear that he too is worshipped and glorified along with the Father and the Son (i.e., he too is fully divine).

The Filioque Debate

One final alteration to the Creed occurred that deserves mention: the addition by the Western church of the Latin word *filioque* ("and the Son") to the clause that said, "And in the Holy Spirit . . . who proceeds from the Father . . ." Accordingly, the clause in the Western church (Catholic and Protestant) now says that the Spirit "proceeds from the Father *and the Son.*" This may seem a trivial matter but it had major ecumenical consequences, as we shall see.

The context was a controversy in sixth-century Spain between the orthodox and Arians. The Arians claimed that the Son was lesser than the Father because the Son was not a source of the Spirit. The Spanish church was rightly keen to defend the essence of Nicene Christology—that Jesus was fully divine—so they introduced, unilaterally, the dual procession of the Spirit from the Father and Son and included it in their Nicene Creed. The theology of the spiration of the Spirit from both the Father and the Son was not new—one finds it very clearly in the influential work of Augustine, for instance—but it was not universally accepted by the bishops so adding it into the ecumenical Creed was, to say the least, problematic.

The use of the Creed with the *filioque* clause spread from Spain to the Frankish Empire and at the Council of Frankfurt (794) the Eastern church were accused of being in error for not including it. However, Pope Leo III (795–816), although he supported the Augustinian theology, urged the Franks to remove the *filioque* from the Creed and had the original Creed engraved in Greek and Latin on silver shields prominently displayed in St. Peter's in Rome.

The *filioque* controversy flared up again in 864, against a background of East and West claiming jurisdiction over Bulgaria. For the first time an Eastern theologian, Patriarch Photius of Constantinople, attacked the West not only for inserting the *filioque* without reference to fellow bishops in the East but argued that the theology underpinning it was wrong. A Council was held in 879–880 and a temporary peace was established and the original Nicene Creed affirmed.

In the eleventh century, however, Pope Benedict VIII allowed the *filioque* to be included in the Creed at an Imperial coronation in Rome; from that time onwards the Roman bishop was no longer commemorated in Constantinople (an estrangement that was in effect a schism). But the other ancient Eastern Sees—Antioch, Alexandria, and Jerusalem—did not blindly follow Byzantium and it was 1100 before we can say the East was of one mind about Rome. From this date onwards the East and West were in *de facto* schism (the 1054 date often quoted as the date of the First Great Schism is somewhat misleading as the process was much more complex and protracted). The Second Council of Lyon (1274) and the Council of Florence (1439) attempted and failed to settle the schism and it remains a reality to this day.

The Eastern objections to the insertion of the word were twofold. First, an objection to the theology they saw implied by it. The Orthodox fear was and is that the dual-source theology puts the Spirit into a subordinate status in the Trinity, potentially threatening his full divine status. Second, an objection to the Pope's claim to have the right to unilaterally approve an alteration to the ecumenical Creed. This papal claim to universal jurisdiction in the church remains a major ongoing cause of disagreement between East and West.

It is important to point out that Western theologians, past and present, are usually clear that they believe that the Spirit's procession from the Father is *different to* his procession from the Son. The Spirit's procession from the Father is to be understood as *primary* and his procession from the Son as *derivative* (the spiration of the Spirit being a capacity that the Father has endowed the Son with). The idea could arguably be put more precisely by saying that the great theologians of the West typically understood that the Spirit proceeds *from* the Father, *through* the Son. And *that* theology is not one that Orthodoxy would oppose for the Spirit's full divinity is not threatened.

Orthodox theologians disagree on whether the *filioque* can be interpreted in such generous ways. And, in their eyes, even if this interpretation of the *filioque* was accepted that would simply move it out of the category of heresy and into the category of *theologoumena*. That is a *very important* move and an important step in ecumenical relations but it is not the same as moving the *filioque* into the category of dogma. As such the Orthodox maintain that it should still not be included in the Creed. For Catholics the *filioque* is dogma with deep roots in the tradition and as such should remain in the Creed.

We can say that the power of Rome and past Western insensitivity to the East was a greater source of tension than the *filioque*. The politics, more than the theology of *filioque*, underlies the schism. This has made the *filioque* clause more, not less significant in that it is the only theological cause of the schism!

APPENDIX 2

Deep Church and Fundamentalism

BEFORE OFFERING SOME WORDS of critique concerning fundamentalism we would like to affirm its intellectual seriousness in its original manifestation at Princeton at the turn of the twentieth century. It seems strange now to think of fundamentalism as a significant intellectual movement. This is because ever since 1925, the year of the infamous Scopes Monkey Trial, fundamentalism has been associated with irrationality, anti-science, and bibliolatry. Indeed, these days fundamentalism is seen as a closed mindset[1] rather than a specific religious ideology; for those people who still associate it with Protestantism *per se* they tend to associate it with wild theories of the apocalypse (as, for instance, in the *Left Behind* series of novels) or a total denial of the possibility of evolution (so-called Creationism, for example). In Princeton, however, under the influence of Archibald A. Hodge (1823–86), the son of the great systematic theologian Charles Hodge (1797–1878), and B. B. Warfield (1851–1921), fundamentalism (as it was later called) was an attempt to follow the lead already given by Vatican I (1869–70) against modernism.

The Princetonian program was based on three ideas: (1) a refusal to accept the Darwinian theory of the origin of the species; (2) a belief that an inspired Bible must be an inerrant Bible (inerrancy was a novel and controversial twist on traditional Christian understandings of Scripture as infallible); and (3) a rejection of Bishop Berkley's idealist theory of common sense in favor of the Scottish common sense philosophy of realist Thomas Reid. The elaborate shape of the Princetonian defense of traditional thinking was an attempt to fit in with the intellectual cultural climate of the late nineteenth century; philosophically speaking, the age was obsessed with

1. See Kaplan, ed., *Fundamentalism* (1992).

epistemological foundationalism and proto-fundamentalism followed suit, simply putting the Bible into the epistemic foundations.

Princetonian fundamentalism was popularized by *The Fundamentals*—twelve volumes published between 1910 and 1915. The authors were conservative intellectuals of the highest order. Some—James Orr, for example—were even somewhat sympathetic to evolution! We need to appreciate that these thinkers opposed scient*ism* and were not anti-science.

However, there was a second wave of fundamentalism, in the early twentieth century, which was the alignment of the Princetonian view of scriptural inerrancy with Cyrus Schofield's Reference Bible (first published in 1909) with its numerous dispensationalist annotations. Schofield's Bible was *hugely influential* and was taken up by most American revivalist movements, including Pentecostals. Dispensationalism damaged the intellectual credibility of fundamentalism, from which it has never really recovered. From our point of view even the wilder and more exotic fundamentalists should really be allies, for unlike the modernists they still support the central tenants of the gospel. Unfortunately they do not prioritize the essential features of gospel truth from secondary and epiphenomenal features of Christian faith. So, for example, speculative theories of eschatology and the theory of inerrancy itself are seen to be as much a test of orthodoxy as the incarnation and the resurrection.

In spite of its early merits and seriousness, the philosophical edifice on which fundamentalism had been built at Princeton was a foundation of sand. The modernist, foundationalist epistemology and the over-confidence in neutral reason were key problems. Putting the Bible into this intellectual framework also generated absurdities. For instance, the doctrine of inerrancy created a need to harmonize all apparent contradictions in the biblical texts. To do this the harmonizers had to go well beyond Scripture. Consider, for example, the attempt to account for the death of Judas: in Matthew Judas hangs himself (27:5) whereas in the Acts of the Apostles we read, "falling headlong, he burst asunder in the midst, and all his bowels gushed out" (1:18; KJV). To explain this apparent contradiction fundamentalists had to invent a story that is not in either Matthew or Acts—that Judas hung himself *but then the rope snapped* and his dead body dropped and split open.

Deep church, although it is conservative, differs from fundamentalism in crucial respects. Having lost a living connection with the Christian tradition, fundamentalism's list of non-negotiable Christian truth—as we have already said—is far too wide. All sorts of issues historically considered by the church to be non-essential or marginal (or even wrong!) were elevated to the status of fundamental truth. Indeed, it was the doctrine of inerrancy that for some fundamentalists made every part of the Bible as important as every other and created Christians willing to die on any hill and to shun other Christians who disagreed with "what God says" (i.e., what our gang interpret the Bible to mean). As a consequence the number of Christian believers accepted as "real believers" was considerably reduced, making fundamentalism deeply sectarian. Not only were Catholics and Orthodox shunned but even many gospel-believing, Bible-affirming Protestants. Deep church, on the other hand, is broad and ecumenical, "deep and wide."

We also think fundamentalism underplays the humanity of Scripture and is in danger of forcing the text to conform to standards imposed on it from without (i.e., the requirement to be 100 percent factually correct in every respect). Biblical texts were indeed Spirit-inspired—this is the faith of the church—but we must not forget that they were written in ordinary human languages by ordinary human beings immersed in ordinary human cultures and histories. Respecting this text requires us to resist forcing it to conform to our pre-fixed categories of what inspired Scripture must be. For instance, biblical authors were not writing to conform to modern Western notions of what truthful history telling should look like. They were happy to narrate the past for the sake of the present, cutting material, relocating material, modifying the wording of material, and even adding what we may call "fictional" material into the blend—all with the goal of truthfully bringing out the *meaning* of the past for the present.[2] The Spirit was working synergistically with the personalities and wills of the human authors. Consequently, these texts wear their humanity very much on their sleeve.

We are rather taken with C. S. Lewis's view that one of the factors that makes the Bible believable is precisely the fact that not everything fits, which, if it did, would suggest the text is fixed. We would rather accept the fact that the Bible has some loose ends that just don't lend themselves to the convolutions of harmonizing texts. So we note that Luke and Mathew's genealogies of Jesus are not the same; we also note that when Peter betrays Jesus the number of times that the cock crows is ambiguous. We also think turning Genesis 1 and 2 into a scientific account of creation is a mistake:

---

2. For a helpful exploration of these questions from an evangelical perspective, see Hays and Ansberry, eds., *Evangelical Faith and the Challenge of Historical Criticism* (2013).

Lewis is surely right in seeing the account of God's creation of the cosmos as prehistory or myth, not science. And does every story in the Old Testament have to be fact? Job and Jonah are surely possible candidates for sacred fiction. Parables told by Jesus are true because of their spiritual prescience not because they are based on fact.

In short, our account of the many and various ways in which the Spirit inspired and guided the diverse parts of the Bible and the long process of its formation cannot be settled *in advance* of engaging the phenomena of the text. That is the mistake of fundamentalism and the consequence is that the Bible is sometimes manhandled to fit the theory. Rather, we contend that we must put our theology of biblical inspiration and authority into an ongoing dialogue with the reality of the text itself so as to rightly receive the Bible that God has given us (as opposed to the one we wish he'd given us). So we read the text in the light of our understanding of biblical inspiration (here fundamentalists are right) but we must also constantly nuance and deepen our understanding of inspiration and authority in the light of the Bible we have and the history of Christian engagement with it.

Bibliography

Anselm. *Proslogion*. In *Anselm of Canterbury: The Major Works*. Oxford World Classics. Edited with an introduction by Brian Davis and G. R. Evans. Reprint. Oxford: Oxford University Press, 1998.

Asad, Talal. "Remarks on the Anthropology of the Body." In *Religion and the Body*, edited by Sarah Coakley, 42–52. Cambridge: Cambridge University Press, 1997.

Bebbington, David W. *Evangelicalism in Modern Britain: A History from the 1730s to the 1980s*. London: Unwin Hyman, 1989.

Bellah, Robert. *Habits of the Heart: Individual Commitment and American Life*. Berkeley: University of California Press, 1985.

Berger, Peter. *The Heretical Imperative: Contemporary Possibilities of Religious Affirmation*. London: Collins, 1980.

———. *The Sacred Canopy: Elements of a Sociological Theory of Religion*. New York: Doubleday, 1967.

Borg, Marcus J. *Jesus: Uncovering the Life, Teachings, and Relevance of a Religious Revolutionary*. 2006. UK ed. London: SPCK, 2011.

Borg, Marcus J., and N. T. Wright. *The Meaning of Jesus: Two Visions*. New York: HarperCollins, 1999.

Bradshaw, Paul. *Early Christian Worship: A Basic Introduction to Ideas and Practice*. London: SPCK, 1996.

Bretherton, Luke. "Beyond the Emerging Church?" In *Remembering Our Future: Explorations in Deep Church*, edited by Andrew Walker and Luke Bretherton, 30–58. Milton Keynes, UK: Paternoster, 2007.

Brotton, Jerry. *The Renaissance: A Very Short Introduction*. Oxford: Oxford University Press, 2006.

Bruce, Steve. *God Is Dead: Secularization in the West*. Oxford: Blackwell, 2002.

Brueggemann, Walter. *Biblical Perspectives on Evangelism: Living in a Three-Storied Universe*. Nashville: Abingdon, 1993.

Bultmann, Rudolf. "New Testament and Mythology: The Mythological Element in the Message of the New Testament and the Problem of its Re-interpretation." In *Kerygma and Myth: A Theological Debate*, edited by Hans Werner Bartsch, translated by Reginald H. Fuller, 1–44. London: SPCK, 1953.

Calvin, John. *Commentary on the Four Last Books of Moses, Arranged in the Form of a Harmony*. Vol. 1. Translated by Charles William Bingham. Grand Rapids: Eerdmans, 1950.

Casanova, José. *Public Religions in the Modern World*. Chicago: University of Chicago Press, 1994.

Cavanaugh, William. *Torture and Eucharist: Theology, Politics and the Body of Christ*. Challenges in Contemporary Theology. Oxford: Wiley-Blackwell, 1998.

Bibliography

Chadwick, Henry. *The Church in Ancient Society: From Galilee to Gregory the Great.* Oxford: Oxford University Press, 2001.

Clapp, Rodney. *Tortured Wonders: Christian Spirituality for People, Not Angels.* Grand Rapids: Brazos, 2004.

Coakley, Sarah. "Beyond Belief." In *The Vocation of Theology: A Festschrift for David Ford,* edited by Tom Greggs et al., 131–45. Eugene, OR: Cascade, 2013.

Costanzo, Eric. *Harbor for the Poor: A Missiological Analysis of Almsgiving in the View and Practice of John Chrysostom.* Eugene, OR: Pickwick, 2013.

Cummings, Owen F. *Eucharist and Ecumenism: The Eucharist across the Ages and Traditions.* Eugene, OR: Pickwick, 2013.

Cupitt, Don. *Creation out of Nothing.* London: SCM, 1989.

———. *Taking Leave of God.* London: SCM, 1980.

Davie, Grace. *Religion in Modern Europe: A Memory Mutates.* Oxford: Oxford University Press, 2000.

———. *The Sociology of Religion.* London: Sage, 2007.

Dawkins, Richard. *The Blind Watchmaker: Why the Evidence of Evolution Reveals a Universe without Design.* London: Penguin, 1986.

Dawn, Marva J. *A Royal "Waste" of Time: The Splendor of Worshipping God and Being Church for the World.* Grand Rapids: Eerdmans, 1999.

Erasmus. Preface to the *Works of Hilary.* (1523). London: n.p., 1642.

Ferber, Michael. *Romanticism: A Very Short Introduction.* Oxford: Oxford University Press, 2010.

Florovsky, Georges. *Bible, Church, Tradition: An Eastern Orthodox View.* Vol. 1 of *The Collected Works of Georges Florovsky.* Belmont, MA: Norland, 1972.

———. "The Function of Tradition in the Ancient Church." In *Bible, Church, Tradition: An Eastern Orthodox View,* 73–92. Belmont, MA: Norland, 1972.

———. "The Lost Scriptural Mind." In *Bible, Church, Tradition: An Eastern Orthodox View,* 9–16. Belmont, MA: Norland, 1972.

Gillespie, Michael Allen. *The Theological Origins of Modernity.* Chicago: Chicago University Press, 2009.

Gorman. Michael. *Cruciformity: Paul's Narrative Spirituality of the Cross.* Grand Rapids: Eerdmans, 2001.

Gregory, Brad S. *The Unintended Reformation: How a Religious Revolution Secularized Society.* Cambridge, MA: Belknap, 2012.

Hanson, Richard P. C. *The Search for the Christian Doctrine of God: The Arian Controversy 318–381.* Edinburgh: T. & T. Clark, 1988.

Hauerwas, Stanley. "How We Lay Bricks and Make Disciples." In *Living Out Loud: Conversations about Virtue, Ethics, and Evangelicalism,* edited by Luke Bretherton and Russell Rook, 39–59. Milton Keynes, UK: Paternoster, 2010.

Hawking, Stephen, and Leonard Mlodinow. *The Grand Design: New Answers to the Ultimate Questions of Life.* London: Bantam, 2010.

Hays, Christopher M., and Christopher B. Ansberry, editors. *Evangelical Faith and the Challenge of Historical Criticism.* London: SPCK, 2013.

Hick, John. *God and the Universe of Faiths.* London: Macmillan, 1973.

———. *An Interpretation of Religion.* London: Macmillan, 1989.

———. *The Metaphor of God Incarnate: Christology in a Pluralistic Age.* London: SCM, 1993.

Hick, John, editor. *The Myth of God Incarnate.* London: SCM, 1977.

Hick, John, and Michael Goulder. *Why Believe in God?* Harrisburg, PA: Trinity, 1983.

Hitchcock, Nathan. *Karl Barth and the Resurrection of the Flesh: The Loss of the Body in Participatory Eschatology.* Eugene, OR: Pickwick, 2013.

Jasper, R. C. D., and G. J. Cummings, editors. *Prayers of the Eucharist: Early and Reformed.* 2nd ed. Oxford: Oxford University Press, 1985.

Johnson, Dru. *Biblical Knowing: A Scriptural Epistemology of Error.* Eugene, OR: Cascade, 2013.

Kant, Immanuel. "An Answer to the Question: What Is Enlightenment?" (1784). In *From Modernism to Postmodernism: An Anthology*, edited by Lawrence Cahoone, 51–57. Oxford: Blackwell, 1996.

———. *Der Streit der Fakultäten.* Vol. 8. Berlin: Reimer, 1917.

Kaplan, Lawrence, editor. *Fundamentalism in Comparative Perspective.* Amherst, MA: University of Massachusetts Press, 1992

Kelly, J. N. D. *Early Christian Doctrines.* 5th rev. ed. London: A. & C. Black, 1977.

Kierkegaard, Søren. *Christian Discourses* and *The Crisis and a Crisis in the Life of an Actress.* Edited and translated by Howard V. Hong and Edna H. Hong. Kierkegaard's Writings 17. Princeton: Princeton University Press, 1997.

———. *The Concept of Anxiety: A Simple Psychologically Orienting Deliberation of the Dogmatic Issue of Hereditary Sin.* Edited and translated by Reidar Thomte. Kierkegaard's Writings 8. Princeton: Princeton University Press, 1981.

———. *Concluding Unscientific Postscript to Philosophical Fragments.* Vol. 1. Edited and trans. Howard V. Hong and Edna H. Hong. Kierkegaard's Writings 12/1. Princeton: Princeton University Press, 1992.

Kreider, Alan. "Baptism and Catechesis as Spiritual Formation." In *Remembering Our Future: Explorations in Deep Church*, edited by Andrew G. Walker and Luke Bretherton, 170–206. Milton Keynes, UK: Paternoster, 2007.

Laytham, D. Brent. *iPod, YouTube, Wii Play: Theological Engagements with Entertainment.* Eugene, OR: Cascade, 2012.

Lewis, C. S. Introduction to *St Athanasius: The Incarnation of the Word. Being the Treatise of St Athanasius, De Incarnationi Verbi Dei.* Translated by Sr. Penelope CSMV. London: Centenary, 1944.

———. "Mere Christians." *Church Times* 135, 8 Feb 1952, 95.

Locke. John. *A Letter Concerning Toleration.* 1689. Edited by James H. Tulley. Indianapolis: Hacket, 1983.

Lossky, Vladimir. *The Mystical Theology of the Eastern Church.* Translated by members of the Fellowship of St. Alban and St. Sergius. London: Clarke, 1957.

Luther, Martin. *That These Words of Christ Still Stand Firm against the Fanatics.* Edited by Robert H. Fischer. Luther's Works 37. Philadelphia: Fortress, 1959.

MacIntyre, Alasdair. *After Virtue: A Study in Moral Theory.* 2nd ed. London: Duckworth, 1985.

MacLaren, Duncan. *Mission Implausible: Restoring Credibility to the Church.* 2004. Reprint. Eugene, OR: Wipf & Stock, 2012.

Martin, David. *A General Theory of Secularization.* Oxford: Blackwell, 1978.

———. *On Secularization: Towards a Revised General Theory.* Aldershot, UK: Ashgate, 2005.

Milbank, John. "Postmodern Critical Augustinianism." In *The Radical Orthodoxy Reader*, edited by John Milbank and Simon Oliver, 49–62. London: Routledge, 2009.

Bibliography

A Monk of the Eastern Church (Fr. Levi Gillet). *Orthodox Spirituality: An Outline of the Orthodox Ascetical and Mystical Tradition*. 2nd ed. 1945. Reprint. London: SPCK, 1978.

Nah, David S. *Christian Theology and Religious Pluralism: A Critical Evaluation of John Hick*. Eugene, OR: Pickwick, 2012.

Nussbaum, Martha. "Non-Relative Virtues: An Aristotelian Approach." In *The Quality of Life*, edited by Martha C. Nussbaum and Amartya Sen, 1–6. Oxford: Clarendon, 1993.

Oden, Thomas. *Rebirth of Orthodoxy: Signs of New Life in Christianity*. San Francisco: HarperSanFranciso, 2003.

Okri, Ben. *Birds of Heaven*. London: Weidenfeld & Nicholson History, 1995.

Parry, Robin A. *Worshipping Trinity: Coming Back to the Heart of Worship*. 2nd ed. Eugene, OR: Cascade, 2012.

Percy, Walker. *Lost in the Cosmos: The Last Self-Help Book*. New York: Farrar, Straus, and Giroux, 1983.

Porter, Thomas. "Learning to Engage Conflict Well." In *Formation for Life: Just Peacemaking and Twenty-First-Century Discipleship*, edited by Glen H. Stassen et al., 147–68. Eugene, OR: Pickwick, 2013.

Principe, Lawrence M. *The Scientific Revolution: A Very Short Introduction*. Oxford: Oxford University Press, 2011.

Proust, Marcel. *The Captive and the Fugitive*. Vol. 5 of *In Search of Lost Time*. Translated by Scott Moncrieff and Terence Kilmartin. Reprint. London: Vintage Classics, 1996.

Putnam, Robert. *Bowling Alone: The Collapse and Revival of American Community*. New York: Simon and Schuster, 2001.

Quick, O. C. *Doctrines of the Creed: Their Basis in Scripture and their Meaning Today*. 1938. Reprint. London: Collins Fontana, 1971.

Ricoeur, Paul. *Time and Narrative*. Vol. 1. Chicago: University of Chicago Press, 1984.

Roberts Kyle. *Emerging Prophet: Kierkegaard and the Postmodern People of God*. Eugene, OR: Cascade, 2013.

Roberts, Robert C. "Narrative Ethics." In *A Companion to the Philosophy of Religion*, edited by P. L. Quinn and C. Taliaferro, 473, 80. Oxford: Blackwell, 1999.

Robinson, J. A. T. *Honest to God*. London: SCM, 1963.

Sinkinson, Christopher. *The Universe of Faiths: A Critical Study of John Hick's Religious Pluralism*. Carlisle, UK: Paternoster, 2001.

Smith, Gordon T. *A Holy Meal: The Lord's Supper in the Life of the Church*. Grand Rapids: Baker Academic, 2005

Stark, R., and W. Bainbridge. *The Future of Religion*. Berkeley: University of California Press, 1985.

———. *A Theory of Religion*. New York: Lang, 1987.

Streett, R. Alan. *Subversive Meals: An Analysis of the Lord's Supper under Roman Domination during the First Century*. Eugene, OR: Pickwick, 2013.

Taylor, Charles. *A Secular Age*. Cambridge, MA: Belknap, 2007.

Thorne, Gary. "Heresy Excludes Itself." *The Living Church*, 20 Jan 2013, 24–25.

Truman, Carl. "The Incarnation and the Lord's Supper." In *The Word Became Flesh: Evangelicals and the Incarnation*, edited by David Peterson, 185–208. Carlisle, UK: Paternoster, 2003.

Vander Zee, Leonard J. *Christ, Baptism, and the Lord's Supper: Recovering the Sacraments for Evangelical Worship*. Downers Grover, IL: InterVarsity, 2004.

Wainwright, Geoffrey. *Eschatology and Eucharist*. 1971. Reprint. Peterborough, UK: Epworth, 2002.

Walker, Andrew G. "The Prophetic Role of Orthodoxy." In *Living Orthodoxy in the Modern World*, edited by Andrew G. Walker and Costa Carras, 217–35. London: SPCK, 1996.

Walker, Andrew G., and Andrew Wright. "A Christian University Imagined." In *The Idea of a Christian University*, edited by Jeff Astley et al., 56–74. Carlisle, UK: Paternoster, 2004.

Ware, Kallistos. "Tradition and Traditions." In *Dictionary of the Ecumenical Movement*, edited by Nicholas Lossky et al., 1013–17. Geneva: WCC, 1991.

Williams, D. H. *Retrieving the Tradition and Renewing Evangelicalism: A Primer for Suspicious Protestants*. Grand Rapids: Eerdmans, 1999.

Williams, Rowan. *Arius: Heresy and Tradition*. Rev. ed. Grand Rapids: Eerdmans, 2002.

World Council of Churches. *Baptism, Eucharist, and Ministry*. Faith and Order Paper 111. Geneva: WCC, 1982.

Wybrew, Hugh. *The Orthodox Liturgy: Development of the Eucharistic Liturgy in the Byzantine Rite*. Crestwood, NY: St Vladimir's Seminary Press, 1992.

Young, Frances. *The Making of the Creeds*. London: SCM, 1991.

Zizioulas, John. *Being as Communion*. Crestwood, NY: St. Vladimir's Seminary Press, 1997.

———. "The Ecclesiological Presuppositions of the Holy Eucharist." In *Eucharistic Communion and the World*, 99–112. London: T. & T. Clark, 2011.

———. "Symbolism and Realism in Orthodox Worship." In *Eucharistic Communion and the World*, 83–98. London: T. & T. Clark, 2011.